The Spirit of Generosity

The Spirit of Generosity

SHAPING IU THROUGH PHILANTHROPY

Curtis R. Simic and Sandra Bate

INDIANA UNIVERSITY PRESS

This book is a publication of

Indiana University Press
Office of Scholarly Publishing
Herman B Wells Library 350
1320 East 10th Street
Bloomington, Indiana 47405 USA

iupress.indiana.edu

This book is printed on acid-free paper.

Manufactured in Canada

Cataloging information is available from the Library of Congress.

ISBN 978-0-253-04329-0 (hardback)
ISBN 978-0-253-04333-7 (ebook)

1 2 3 4 5   24 23 22 21 20 19

Contents

Preface

I have long believed that life's most important facet is relationships—between nations, between cultures, between spouses, between parents and children. The inspiring world of philanthropy flourishes because of relationships between donors and the causes they support.

Every significant advance Indiana University has navigated since its very founding in 1820 has been infused with and propelled by gifts, both the remarkably large gifts and the many, many smaller gifts given by thousands of people each year. And, over the past half century, those gift dollars have dramatically augmented the impact of the state of Indiana's appropriations and the tuition and fees IU students pay. Often, each of these three sources of support have encouraged one another because of their alignment with the University's needs, aspirations, and desired impact.

The essays that follow speak specifically to what philanthropists found compelling about building a partnership with Indiana University to advance the common good. My mentor and friend at the University of Oregon, President William Beaty Boyd, put it this way: "Scholarship and philanthropy are each, separately, among the most powerful forces at work shaping the future of our society. In combination, they may be unsurpassed in their capacity to improve the human condition."

The dream of improving the human condition is why people choose to invest in Indiana University. It is simply astounding to observe tens of thousands of individuals stepping forward to make something good happen. As this generosity of spirit advances across our nation, our state, and our communities, one cannot help but be both inspired and hopeful.

There is a solemn pact established between each donor and Indiana University when a gift is made. It's an expectation that IU will deliver on its commitment. It's a confidence that there will be fulfillment of the University's ambition to create what has been proposed, that this creation will have an impact, and that the partnership will generate both progress and satisfaction. Whether it is discovering new knowledge, passing knowledge on to students, or seeing new applications of knowledge, the allure of giving to support a young person's journey and serve the common good is unparalleled.

In these essays, Sandra Bate and I have focused on the motivation and impact of benefactors who have made investments in the people, programs, and places that define Indiana University. How did a commitment become so great that it prompted action? What was the motivation? Loyalty? An appreciation of one's own IU experience? Fond, lifelong memories of peers and mentors? Aspiration to change the world through research, teaching, or service?

As IU approaches its bicentennial, we wanted to ensure that the generosity of spirit that has shaped the character and impact of Indiana University is never forgotten. Each of the thirteen profiles here tells a different story of partnership. These few could have been hundreds—indeed, each day I think of several more people I have worked with whose stories could be told. With that recognition, we moved ahead with what you hold here. It is our hope that you will feel a sense of shared pride and an appreciation for how each sought to advance the common good at Indiana University and far beyond.

Curtis R. Simic

JANUARY 2018
BLOOMINGTON, INDIANA

Acknowledgments

Without the thirteen benefactors whose giving created legacies at Indiana University, we would have had no stories to tell about the extraordinary philanthropy that has shaped the university through the years.

So, our first thank you goes to Gayle Cook, Sid Eskenazi, Lucie Glaubinger, Bill Hunt, David Jacobs, Pat Miller, Cindy Simon Skjodt, and Mary Margaret Webb. You welcomed us to your homes and offices or came to visit us in Bloomington. Thank you for your gifts of time.

Other colleagues and friends generously made time to talk with us and help detail the significance of giving in the lives of several deceased benefactors. To Betty Lofton, Clay Robbins, Tom McGlasson, Kent Dove, Eileen Savage, Alan Gilman, and Sandy Laney, we are grateful for your sharing of your rich memories.

At the Indiana University Foundation, our former colleagues helped document facts and figures and searched diligently for portraits and photographs.

Kenya Cockerham, Melissa Fulton, and Sherri Knieriem, as always, your work consistently advances Indiana University. Thank you.

Tyagan Miller brought a camera out of retirement for a few days and went back to the Bloomington campus to produce several new striking images for us.

Terry Clapacs, our trusted friend and vice president emeritus of Indiana University, shared his firsthand knowledge of IU's eight campuses and quickly responded to our requests for clarification and detail.

Gary Dunham and Peggy Solic at the Indiana University Press have led, cajoled, and inspired us. We thank them both.

And to the many others in the Indiana University schools and departments statewide whose assistance was critical to our work, we thank you for what you do to perpetuate the generosity and giving that distinguish this grand university today.

Following
Sample Gates, Indiana University Bloomington. *Photo: James Brosher and Eric Rudd, Indiana University Communications*

The Spirit of Generosity

A
Commitment to
Opportunity

PROVIDING BROAD ACCESS

TO EDUCATION AT

INDIANA UNIVERSITY

Indiana University's beloved chancellor emeritus Herman B Wells loved to quote an ancient Chinese proverb: "If you are planning for a year ahead . . . sow rice. For ten years . . . plant trees. For a hundred years . . . educate people."

Since the 1636 founding of Harvard, America's first college, the task of offering education to people has included, at its very core, the need to ensure broad access to opportunity. The most superior and beautiful campus, the most highly qualified teaching faculty, the most inspiring curricula are only significant when students have access to the promise of what those components of a university can bring to their lives.

Providing that broad access through scholarships and fellowships is a philanthropic mission that has consistently appealed to Indiana University's most generous donors. In fact, it is not uncommon to find that many donors first give to scholarship programs, beginning their own philanthropic journeys to open doors of opportunity.

Through gifts that endow financial aid programs, these benefactors assure that today's students will gain from the wisdom and expertise epitomized on a university campus to prepare for lives of leadership in tomorrow's global economy.

*Photo: Indiana University
Foundation*

JESSE H. COX

Of Knowledge, Hard Work, and Self-Confidence

Like others in his generation who experienced the Great Depression firsthand, Jesse H. Cox valued the basics in life: knowledge, hard work, and discipline. And he regarded self-confidence as one of life's essentials.

A 1944 graduate of Indiana University, Jesse might rightfully be called one of his alma mater's most quotable alumni. He stated things plainly, to the point, with little fanfare:

· You expect success and it happens.
· The way to build confidence is to do everything you can the very best that you can do it.
· You exude confidence, and people are willing to do, or help you do, what you say you're going to do.

· Accumulated knowledge is the greatest key to a future of happiness.

Late in his life, after he had given the largest gift in Indiana University history to fund student scholarships, Jesse met with the first selected group of Cox Scholars. These were the first students for whom a college education would become a reality because of Jesse's generosity.

Jesse was, characteristically, quite quotable that day. In a conference room on the Indiana University Purdue University Indianapolis (IUPUI) campus, he walked to the podium wearing his IU cap, looked out at the dozen or so young faces before him, and said, "I've been thinking about you since before you were born."

Seasons of Giving Back. Each spring, Indiana University Cox Scholars volunteer to travel to Coxhall Gardens to give back, in kind, to Jesse and Beulah Cox. Here, Cox Scholars (*l–r*) Fatjona Hasani, Casey Stover, and Gbemisola Owolabi take a break during the workday to clean up the park and get it ready for the coming season. The park was a 125-acre gift from the Coxes to preserve an oasis of open spaces, water, and gardens in southwestern Hamilton County. *Photo: Cox Scholars Program, Indiana University*

Those gathered that day to meet Jesse Cox sensed the authenticity of the man who, through his remarkable philanthropy, made a gift that now assists nearly four hundred students each year at Indiana University.

WORKING HIS WAY

Jesse Cox was born in 1918 in Utah, where his parents had been lured from Indiana by offers of cheap land during the years leading up to the Depression. But the family returned to the Hoosier state when Jesse was only four, and a short two years later, according to his own account, Jesse started working on the family farm.

Farming, and the land itself, were in his blood. In fact, years and years later, as a business magnate, Jesse farmed again, driving his own tractor and growing crops on his own land.

After his high school graduation in Indianapolis, Jesse was equally eager for employment and more education. He went to work immediately and enrolled first at Indiana Central Business College and then Butler University on a part-time basis at night. His high school sweetheart, Beulah Chanley, also had enrolled at and eventually graduated from the business college in Indianapolis.

Jesse arrived in Bloomington in 1939 and entered Indiana University that fall. He and Beulah were married the same year, and Jesse went to work immediately in Bloomington to earn his way through school.

First was a transportation business. Jesse had saved three hundred dollars for college from his work in Indianapolis. He purchased two used Model A Fords when he arrived at IU to set up his own Bloomington-to-Indianapolis car service. "I was a good mechanic," Jesse explained, "especially on old cars, because that's all we ever owned."

After getting the cars up and running, Jesse posted signs all over campus, promoting trips to and from the capital city. "I drove one car, and a friend drove the other back and forth. A trip was one dollar and fifty cents per person," Jesse said.

Business was good because students needed transportation to get to bus and rail stations in Indianapolis. But one day, the IU dean of men tracked Jesse down and asked, "Are you the young guy with these signs all over campus for Naptown transportation?"

"Yes," Jesse said. And the dean promptly began a litany of the legal necessities required to provide public transportation. Liability insurance was near the top of the list, but Jesse later acknowledged that he "hardly knew what that meant."

But he was readily convinced of his legal risks, so he went around campus, took the signs down, and quickly sold one of the Model As. "But I kept the better one," he said.

With the funds from the sale of the car, he purchased a mimeograph machine and began printing

I never met Jesse Cox. I will never get to tell him how thankful I am for what he has done for me and many others. But I feel like I know him well, and he will continue to inspire me every day.

Alexea Candreva
IU Class of 2015,
Cox Scholar

newsletters, handbills, and posters. "I never hesitated to take my last thirty dollars and buy that mimeograph machine," Jesse said, "because I never had any doubt that I was going to get work for that machine."

That's the kind of confidence that distinguished Jesse Cox through his IU days and into his young business career.

EVER INQUISITIVE

Jesse served in the US Army after the outbreak of World War II, and thus, his graduation from IU was delayed a year until 1944. He was stationed at Fort Benjamin Harrison, northeast of Indianapolis, as a member of the Quartermaster Corps.

When Jesse graduated in 1944, he and Beulah started the J. H. Cox Manufacturing Co. to supply venetian blinds to top retailers like Sears & Roebuck, L. S. Ayres, and William H. Block.

Why venetian blinds? Two reasons, most likely. First, Jesse, as a member of the Quartermaster Corps, was experienced in producing supplies that were essential to support soldiers on military bases. That experience included décor of barracks and structures, to the degree that "décor" existed on Army bases.

Second, he saw an opportunity. And he discovered the opportunity because he was a voracious reader.

"Studious and well-read. Very, very well-read." That's the description of Jesse Cox offered by Tom McGlasson, a Bloomington attorney and longtime legal counsel to Jesse.

"Books, newspapers, magazines. He read *Barron's* religiously. He was ever inquisitive. And if Mr. Cox read a book that he liked and he thought you or another person should read it, he would buy a box of those books. The next time he saw you, he'd say, 'Here, I think you ought to read this,'" Tom said.

"A month or so later when he saw you, he'd ask, 'Well, what did you think of the book?'"

"You learned quickly," Tom said, "to read what Mr. Cox passed on to you."

Reading the *Chicago Tribune* one day, Jesse saw an advertisement for a punch machine that drilled holes for venetian blinds. Intrigued by the possibilities, the young IU graduate explored how the punch could be used to manufacture blinds more economically and more profitably. He learned about the processes, and the Coxes soon had a business manufacturing blinds.

Quite quickly, Jesse and Beulah expanded their young enterprise to draperies and window coverings. The next step was to buy a small bankrupt company and begin Aero Blind & Drapery, Inc. When Aero was sold in 1982, there were over nine hundred employees and annual sales of more than thirty million dollars.

Jesse's love of the land prompted another business venture for the entrepreneur—a land and real estate rental company. Hiring tenant farmers, he farmed nearly 1,500 acres in Boone, Hamilton, and Putnam counties surrounding Indianapolis and also owned and managed rental properties across the state.

A Commitment to Opportunity

Tom McGlasson, who graduated from IU in 1965 and received his IU law degree in 1968, had a longstanding friendship with Jesse. Tom was vice-president and general counsel at the Indiana University Foundation prior to entering private law practice in Bloomington. He first met Jesse and Beulah Cox when they called the Indiana University Foundation and stated that they would "like to make a gift to IU."

At the time, Jesse was beginning to downsize some of his real estate holdings. He explained to Tom that he had a dream to help students achieve a college education at Indiana University.

"So we went to see him," Tom said.

After their original meeting, Tom said it was clear that Jesse had been thinking about how he wanted his gift to have an impact on IU students. Tom introduced Jesse and Beulah to the director of scholarships and financial aid at Indiana University, Ed Sample. And, as often happens with such introductions, what ensued was a series of conversations that helped the Coxes clarify their thinking about their giving to IU.

First, they determined, they wanted to assist Indiana residents. Next, they wanted to require a certain grade point average (GPA) to ensure the students were both capable and hard working. And, most critically, Jesse and Beulah wanted to focus their philanthropy on students who—like Jesse—had to work hard to put themselves through school.

"Mr. Cox had determined to do something to give those hard workers one of the biggest boosts they'd ever receive in life," Tom said.

"YOU NEED TO MEET THESE KIDS"

The discussions between the Coxes and Indiana University were the genesis of the landmark Cox Scholars Program. "We put together a flexible document as a gift agreement for Mr. Cox, and it served his purposes well," Tom said.

To ensure they would assist those who most needed it, Jesse stipulated that scholarship recipients had to work to contribute at least 25 percent of the standard cost of their attendance at IU throughout their college careers.

But after the agreement was drafted, Jesse expressed a primary concern: "Now you know, I don't want any publicity about this. I don't want my name involved." So he said, "Let's not activate this right now. Let's just hold on the activation because I don't want the publicity."

The gift had been outlined and approved by Jesse to accomplish exactly what he had in mind. And then, in line with his preference to avoid publicity, it was set aside for implementation upon his death.

An invitation from Curt Simic, president of the Indiana University Foundation at the time, prompted Jesse to re-consider that "hold."

"It was becoming clearer and clearer to me that Jesse was making a most remarkable commitment to

THE IMPORTANCE OF TRUST

Sometimes, donors dream dreams they may not know how to achieve. That's where advisors and experts come in.

Tom McGlasson, a native Hoosier with two Indiana University degrees, worked for more than twenty years at the Indiana University Foundation. Through those years, he met innumerable individuals who wanted to make gifts to IU. "Most had strong inclinations about what they wanted to accomplish with their gifts but needed guidance on how to get the tasks done," Tom said.

Jesse Cox was one of those donors. He called the IU Foundation when he and his wife first decided to make a gift to fund scholarships. Tom and other IUF staff met with Mr. Cox. Tom soon became an advisor about the best way for the Coxes to accomplish their goals.

"Trust is awfully important at this stage," Tom said. "And that is built through relationships that grow through the years."

After Tom left the IU Foundation in 1993 to join a small law firm in Bloomington, Mr. Cox asked him to become his personal attorney. Mr. Cox's own attorney had retired, leaving him looking for new counsel.

"When a donor says, 'I want to . . .' you take your lead and begin to identify ways to help him implement his dreams," Tom said. With Mr. Cox, this meant a twenty-two-year relationship that involved putting in place a flexible plan for him to accomplish his intentions.

And IU students, today and in perpetuity, are the beneficiaries of both that plan and that relationship. Tom said, "When I meet these Cox Scholars each year at graduation and tell them a little about Jesse Cox, I am so proud to say,

'This man cared about you and your success.'"

the IU students who were going to make, likewise, remarkable commitments to put themselves through school. I told him one day that I'd love for him to meet those kids so he could understand what exactly his giving would mean to them," Curt said.

And Jesse agreed. Sitting at a table in the McGlasson law firm in Bloomington, he agreed to the idea of meeting the first group of Cox Scholars. His reaction? "Well, this is not such a bad idea."

And he added, "If this works, you know, there is more where that came from. The contribution I can make now is to enable people to make their contributions."

While some philanthropists reward great achievements, others express their generosity of spirit by rewarding great promise. Jesse Cox's experiences in life . . . led him to believe that it takes special determination, special drive, special ambition, to realize the dream of a college education, especially at a campus like IUPUI, where most students work. The Cox Scholarships reward promise and hard work and ultimately fulfill dreams.

Charles Bantz
IU Executive Vice President and Chancellor, Indiana University Purdue University Indianapolis

A FOCUS ON DONOR INTENT

The evolution and maturation of the Cox Scholars Program at Indiana University is one of the most extraordinary stories of how a precise focus on a donor's intention can actually broaden a program to fully realize its impact.

Jesse had great affection for the Bloomington campus of Indiana University. But his commitment to working students soon prompted a conversation about the possibility of expanding the Cox Scholars program to students at IUPUI.

"One day Jesse and I were talking, and he mentioned that some of his extended family members had taken courses at IUPUI. I asked whether he had ever thought about giving to IUPUI because so many of our students there are working students," Curt said.

"Well, what do you have in mind?" Jesse asked. Curt offered Jesse a profile of the IUPUI student body, indicating how many local students attended IUPUI and how many were employed full- or part-time. The two talked about possibilities and came to the conclusion that one-third of the original gift for scholarships would be dedicated to IUPUI students and two-thirds to Bloomington students.

And then another conversation occurred. William Plater, then executive vice chancellor and dean of the faculties at IUPUI, told Curt about a situation developing on the Indianapolis campus.

IUPUI enrolled students either as Indiana University or Purdue University students. In the early years of the Cox Scholars program, some students—desperate for funding for their college education—were considering transferring out of Purdue programs into IU programs to qualify for the scholarships. Again, Curt and Jesse sat down to discuss options.

When Jesse met Purdue students from the IUPUI campus, Curt said, he was so impressed with their initiative and commitment to hard work that he decided to expand the program so Purdue students at IUPUI could qualify as Cox Scholars.

At first, students selected through the rigorous application process to receive scholarships were called, simply, Cox Scholars. Now, on the IU Bloomington campus, because of the resources from the Cox gift, there have been five new programs added, resulting in this lineup of opportunities for IU Bloomington students:

· Cox Access Scholars Program provides opportunity for students who are returning to school after a gap of five years or more in their college education.
· Cox Civic Scholars Program provides opportunity for incoming freshmen to connect IU students to volunteer at local nonprofits.
· Cox Engagement Scholars Program provides opportunity for students to make a commitment to community service.
· Cox Exploratory Scholars Program provides opportunity for students to work hands-on to help educate and mentor their IU peers.
· Cox Legacy Scholars Program, the original Cox Scholars, provides opportunity for academically strong Indiana residents to receive assistance when they earn a share of the cost of their education.

Jesse was an inspiration to all who believe that happiness can be found in the quest for knowledge and that a strong work ethic deserves to be rewarded. His support, service, and generosity have had a profound impact on Indiana University and higher education in Indiana.

Michael A. McRobbie
President,
Indiana University

· Cox Research Scholars Program provides opportunity for students to participate in meaningful research or creative activity under faculty mentorship.

A comparison between the first year of the Cox Scholars Program and the most recent academic year indicates remarkable growth. In 2005 at IUPUI there were seven students enrolled in the program; in 2017–18, one hundred students were enrolled. At IU Bloomington, fourteen students began the program in 2005, and in 2017–18, 285 were enrolled.

This is not a scholarship in which you are simply handed money. We all work hard for the money we are being given, whether it's giving back and helping other students connect with the community, gaining knowledge by discovering different aspects of campus, working a part-time job, or conducting meaningful research.

Alexea Candreva
IU Class of 2015, Cox Scholar

The gift originally given by Jesse and Beulah Cox in 1989 and designated for scholarships was invested and not utilized to start the Cox Scholars program until 2005. The funds grew along with other gifts from the Coxes over the next sixteen years and remained anonymous, according to Jesse's expressed preferences.

When public announcement was made in 2005 and the first scholarships were awarded, it became clear that Jesse was energized by his contact with IU students who had been selected for the first Cox Scholars class.

Indiana University, at the time, was in the midst of a fundraising campaign that offered a university match for gifts that were fully funded and, thus, irrevocable. When Jesse learned about the match possibility, he asked Curt Simic, "Are you telling me that my program could be twice as large and offer twice as many scholarships?"

"Yes," Curt told Jesse. "That's exactly right."

Jesse, ever the good business man who saw the advantage of moving quickly, said to Curt, "You better come see me."

The estate gift was announced in December 2008, following Jesse's death earlier that year, as the largest individual gift in IU's history and the largest gift ever given for scholarships.

NEW PERSPECTIVE
JOSHUA MULLET

"I scoffed at the idea of going to college when I was growing up. I had no interest, primarily because of the financial weight of a college degree."

That's the introduction Joshua Mullet, an IU Class of 2017 computer science major, offers in a discussion about being a Cox Scholar at Indiana University. "I couldn't have been more wrong," he frankly admits.

"The friendships, the experiences, the personal growth— these are the things I was allowed to enjoy on a grand scale. And, I was able to identify and develop my skills with com-puters. I can confidently say that I am infinitely better prepared for the workforce because of my time at IU," Joshua said.

To earn his share of the total cost of his education, Joshua worked in the IU Physics Department as a freshman and as a peer mentor and coach during his last three years in school.

"I came to college because of the generosity of people I never met. It is humbling to realize that I am only an IU graduate today because of the invisible hand of so many others," Joshua said.

"When donors choose to invest in a program like the Cox Scholars, people like me are transported from a place without the means of going to college to graduation with a strong degree and a grand chance for success," Joshua concluded.

LIFE-CHANGING
ERICA WHALEN

Erica Whalen, who received her dual degree in communication studies and journalism at Indiana University Purdue University Indianapolis (IUPUI) in 2017, is one of those students who would have made Jesse Cox smile.

Erica, like Jesse, worked—and worked hard—to earn her college degree. Throughout her college days, she maintained three jobs simultaneously, working as a restaurant server, a childcare center assistant, and in one of four internships she completed as an undergraduate. Erica's internships were done at Emmis Communications, WISH TV News, Eli Lilly and Company, and Dittoe Public Relations.

"Receiving the Cox Scholarship had a most significant impact on my character," Erica said, "and I now view life from a new perspective because I realize that hard work does pay off."

Erica was married a month after graduation, and she and her new husband are now living in San Francisco. Her Cox Scholarship was "the most life-changing and humbling scholarship I could have been awarded," she said.

"Our founders were the most selfless and kind people, and their legacy and story live on with the scholars today," she added.

It's hard to express my appreciation for the fact that I was the recipient of an award that offers education and opportunity to students who could not otherwise afford it. I can only hope that in my time after graduation, I will be able to expand opportunity to students in the same way that the Cox Scholars program did for me.

Dennis Coffey
IU Class of 2017, Cox Scholar

Jesse and Beulah loved IU, and they loved Bloomington. Often, in their later years, they would call Tom McGlasson and say, "Well, we don't have anything to do today, so we are going to drive down to Bloomington. Are you free for an hour?"

"Yes," Tom would say. And soon the Coxes were there, asking Tom if he wanted to have lunch at Bob Evans on the west side of Bloomington. Jesse, Tom explained, owned stock in Bob Evans, so "we ate there quite frequently."

Jesse and Beulah loved walking the IU campus and especially enjoyed the arboretum behind the Herman B Wells Library. One of their gifts funded an irrigation system and continuing maintenance of the pavilion in the arboretum. In their honor, the arboretum was renamed the Jesse H. and Beulah Chanley Cox Arboretum.

The Coxes also loved to dance. Their home on 116th Street in Indianapolis had four floors, with a ballroom at the top. Jesse had a jukebox up in the ballroom, and he and Beulah would host parties there and dance to the tunes of the '40s and '50s. The Coxes eventually donated their home and the surrounding 125 acres of land to the Hamilton County Parks and Recreation Department to "preserve an oasis in a sea of housing."

Beulah Cox died in 1999, shortly after she and Jesse celebrated their sixtieth wedding anniversary. Jesse died at the age of ninety, in May 2008, just a few days after he attended the graduation ceremonies of the first class of Cox Scholars at IUPUI.

"Jesse saw his dream come true," Curt said. "He believed in education. He believed in hard work. He believed in opportunity and a hand up. So for him, his long-term contribution to life was to help educate the students of the next generation so they could make their contributions to the world."

Curt has no doubt that his longtime friend died a happy man. In his inimitable style, Jesse once asked Curt, "What's wealth for? There's great happiness in being able to share it."

These are wonderful gifts from generous donors who knew that higher education is the key to the future, both for the individuals receiving the scholarships and for us—the citizens of the state, the nation, and the world.

Curt Simic
President Emeritus,
Indiana University Foundation

Photo: Indiana University Foundation

LUCIENNE &LAWRENCE GLAUBINGER

An Investment in People

A thletes and curators. Promising entrepreneurs. Graduate assistants. Wells Scholars.

The people at Indiana University who benefit today from the generosity of Lucienne and Lawrence Glaubinger are, indeed, a varied lot. In this special group of recipients of philanthropy, you'll find varsity athletes who row, swim, race, jump—or, in fact, participate in any intercollegiate sport but football or basketball.

There are IU art administrators who plan, administer, and supervise the respected collection of the IU Eskenazi Museum of Art. And, of course, there are Wells Scholars, students who receive one of the most competitive and prestigious scholarships offered by any American university.

These are the people who today—because of gifts to Indiana University since the early 1980s by Larry and Lucie Glaubinger—study, compete, engage, re-search, and enhance quality of life in a host of fields around the globe. These are the people who were planned for when Larry and Lucie dedicated their philanthropy to the future at Indiana University.

THE ATTRACTION OF OPPOSITES

Larry and Lucie Glaubinger, in some ways, appear to prove the "opposites attract" theory. She was a Canadian, born in Iroquois Falls, Ontario; he was born in Newark, New Jersey. She was soft-spoken, with a warm smile. Larry was deliberate and outspoken.

"It was difficult to *mis*understand Larry," Curt Simic, president emeritus of the Indiana University Foundation, says of the former member of the IU Foundation Board of Directors. Lucie adds, "Larry was always an outspoken person. He would never mislead you."

Go Hoosiers! Athletes on the Indiana University Rowing Team are among competitors in twenty-two Olympic varsity sports who may qualify for Glaubinger Scholar-Athlete scholarships. The rowing team practices on Lake Lemon, a few miles east of the Bloomington campus. *Photo: Tyagan Miller*

Larry and Lucie did indeed have interests as varying as their countries of origin. They met through friends at a party for the textile industry. So goes the story. Their wedding was three years later on Armistice Day, November 11, 1967. "We called a truce, I guess," Lucie said.

At the time of their wedding, Lucie was an airline hostess, working international routes for TWA and traveling regularly between JFK and Paris, London, Los Angeles, and four other points in Europe.

International travel brought international exposure to life and art for Lucie and fed her love of seeing exceptional works of art and collecting special pieces, some of which still sit in her New York City living room today. "I was not educated in art," Lucie said, "but as I educated my eye, I began to know what I liked."

That 1960s interest in art manifests itself, today, in Lucie's partnership in the Montreal gallery, Beaux Arts des Amériques, which she founded in 2007 with Jacqueline Stoneberger, a lifelong friend.

AN ENTREPRENEUR FROM THE START

Larry was stationed in the South Pacific with the US Coast Guard during the final days of World War II. When he got out of the service, he enrolled at a junior college in Pennsylvania and played baseball and basketball. It was his hope, he explained, to transfer to Penn.

"But Penn wanted me to start over as a freshman. Then I heard from Indiana that they would accept me without starting over. So it was Indiana," he said in a 2006 interview. And the GI Bill paid his way, opening the door to a highly valued university experience that led to a successful career in the business world of New York City.

Larry graduated, with distinction, from Indiana University in 1949 with a degree in accounting. He never worked, though, as a practicing accountant. "I got a job as a sales trainee with United Merchants, a public textile company," Larry said. He worked his way up to become manager of the imported fabrics department, but then he left the company "over some changes I didn't agree with," he said.

He soon joined another textile company that was a family-owned business. And Larry Glaubinger the entrepreneur began his own career in earnest then.

"After a while I had to go to the owner and tell him that he did not have the resources to do what he had hired me to do. I advised him to forget about apparel textiles and concentrate on his more profitable division," Larry said.

"When the owner was ready to liquidate his apparel textile assets, I started a company to buy his inventory—Channel Textile Company, Inc.," Larry explained.

After nine years, he sold his share of Channel to his business partner, and Larry settled on his next move: "I wanted to teach college, so I enrolled in the business PhD program at Columbia University in New York City."

The academic program was not what Larry had expected and, most likely, was a bit too removed from hands-on entrepreneurship. So after a year, he told Lucie that he didn't want to be teacher after all, took his MBA degree at Columbia in 1977, and moved on.

Next was a leveraged buyout of another company, and Larry then proceeded to take Stern & Stern private and into the position of one of the country's leading manufacturers of fabrics for industrial applications, including aerospace and outer space usage.

NEW SHARED WORLDS

Early into their marriage, Larry introduced Lucie to two worlds completely new to her: the textile industry and Indiana University.

One introduction occurred in the offices of Larry's company, where Lucie sometimes helped when she was off duty from TWA.

The second introduction was to Indiana University in Bloomington. There's something to those age-old adages about Hoosier hospitality, Lucie says. "The people in Indiana were so pleasant and welcoming," she explained. "I learned to really like visiting Bloomington."

The Glaubingers traveled to Indiana University frequently over the years. For Larry, part of the attraction was IU basketball and football. Lucie says, "I attended the games when I had to," but then found other opportunities for much more interesting engagement on the Bloomington campus.

Larry served on the boards of directors of the Indiana University Foundation and the Indiana University Varsity Club and was also a member of the Dean's Advisory Council of the Kelley School of Business.

Lucie was invited by then director Adelheid (Heidi) Gealt to serve on the National Advisory Board of the Indiana University Eskenazi Museum of Art. Heidi recalls organizing the Advisory Board to gain financial support, advice, and advocacy. And all three tasks were critical ones for the maturation of the IU museum, Heidi said.

When the first Advisory Board was organized, there were no endowments for the museum. By the time Heidi retired in 2015, there was an endowment of more than $15 million, plus a good number of planned gifts that had been promised to grow the endowment.

Lucie and Larry Glaubinger were among the donors who chose to contribute to that essential endowment. In each instance, Heidi said, "We had nothing, and suddenly because of exceptionally committed benefactors like Lucie and Larry, we had significant amounts of money to endow our leadership positions."

Through their philanthropy over the years at Indiana University, Lucie and Larry shared a common objective: to invest in people. For Larry, that meant, among other priorities, establishing scholarship funds to benefit student-athletes in non-revenue varsity sports.

Lucie Glaubinger had been invited to the Indiana University Eskenazi Museum of Art for a private tour. At the tour's completion, the guests were walking into a conference room for a short presentation.

"We had this door stop and it wouldn't work, so we couldn't keep the door open," recalls the Eskenazi Museum of Art director emerita Heidi Gealt.

Nonetheless, the tour concluded, and Lucie returned to her home in New York City. Soon, via mail, a special package arrived in Heidi's mailbox from Lucie. "It was a metal doorstop and it was on a spring, so it would wedge itself to exactly the right dimension between the bottom of the door and the floor," Heidi said.

"I used to call it the Lucie Glaubinger Memorial Door Stop because we kept it from then on. It was just so thoughtful of Lucie to send it, and it was very functional, which is so classic Lucie," Heidi added.

Functionality and advocacy. For Heidi Gealt and Indiana University, when Lucie Glaubinger joined the Eskenazi Museum of Art's first National Advisory Board, the museum got both.

Lucie, Heidi recalls, was perfect as an advisory board member: "For a long time I called her our documentarian because she would take photographs during board meetings and send them to other members. She reached out to everyone and became engaged very quickly. She was one of the cornerstones who held that board together."

Donors serving in an advisory capacity quickly develop an informed awareness of an institution and its needs, Heidi said.

"I never really asked our board members to give to certain funds. Rather, they would hear about how we were doing and about the needs we had. Later, they would come to me privately and say, 'We'd like to do that.'"

Heidi, who retired as director of the IU Eskenazi Museum of Art in 2015, said, "You build the relationships and the relationships blossom with gifts to meet needs. This kind of fundraising is based on relationships that last forever."

And, inevitably, the relationships branch out and extend their influence. Barry Gealt, Heidi's husband and a longtime member of the IU School of Fine Arts faculty, founded the Italy study abroad program for art students. Larry and Lucie learned about the new option and were quite impressed with the opportunity it provided students. Larry eventually told Barry, "The next time you need scholarships, let us know."

Barry did, and the Glaubingers gave Indiana University several art scholarships.

"In addition to the financial support that engaged board members bring to your program, there is tremendous benefit in the goodwill of good relationships. That forms a network of association that spreads positive messaging," Heidi explained.

"Your reputation can be built by hiring a PR firm, for sure. But that's not nearly as powerful or as influential as the network of good relationships that you have with respected people who love you.

"With Lucie and so many other friends we've made at the museum, their goodwill crosses the world. That is worth its weight in gold."

"I am a firm believer in the term 'student-athlete'" Larry said, "and I want to help benefit both academics and athletics at Indiana University."

In 2005, the Glaubingers made a major commitment to IU Athletics to provide scholarships for IU Bloomington student-athletes who participate in twenty-two Olympic non-revenue varsity sports. Each year since, a select group of both male and female athletes are designated as Glaubinger Scholar-Athletes.

This unprecedented gift . . . will help ensure that the ultimate end-users, our student-athletes, can continue to succeed on and off the playing fields to further IU's tradition of excellence. The legacy of this gift, and the hundreds of student-athletes it will serve, will not be long forgotten.

Ron Remak
President, Indiana University Varsity Club
National Board of Directors

Like many major gifts given to Indiana University at opportune times, Larry and Lucie's gift qualified for matching funds through a fundraising campaign that was underway on the Bloomington campus, Matching the Promise. This institutional match, commonly a special feature of capital campaigns in higher education, essentially doubles the impact of the gifts made during matching campaigns.

We are delighted that the campus can match the income of this gift in perpetuity, effectively doubling the impact of its financial support. Larry and Lucie epitomize what giving back really means.

Kenneth Gros Louis
Bloomington Chancellor and Vice President for Academic Affairs

Lucie chose carefully to designate her gifts to areas of special appeal to her. "I am not interested in building buildings. I have always stipulated that our IU gifts go to fund people in art and education," she said.

Specifically, because she wanted to assure continuity and excellence in the management of the Indiana University Eskenazi Museum of Art, she funded the establishment of two endowments.

The first supports the museum's Works on Paper Department. The Lucienne M. Glaubinger Curatorship for Works on Paper provides funding to support the curator in this area, which includes more than half of the museum's forty-five thousand objects.

The second endowment funds the Lucienne M. Glaubinger Curatorship for Education. In the past fiscal year, the museum's education department conducted a total of 1,244 tours for more than 17,000 people, including some 4,700 K–12 students. The Glaubinger Curatorship endowment funds teacher training, resource materials, family days, and a portion of

A Commitment to Opportunity

the schools' bus transportation costs to and from the Eskenazi Museum of Art.

Larry Glaubinger's interest in business and his own identity as the quintessential entrepreneur were certainly motivators for another series of gifts made by the couple to Indiana University. They funded six scholarships for resident entrepreneurship majors and two for non-residents in the Kelley School of Business; the awards were made for the first time in the 2001 fall semester.

ESSENTIAL GENEROSITY

From athletes who learn about competition in both gyms and classrooms to curators who keep the complicated parts of a university museum synchronized and moving forward . . . from future entrepreneurs and business leaders to graduate students, public school students, and art teachers . . . the people at Indiana University and those touched by IU are the recipients, over and over again, of Lucie's and Larry's generosity.

Through their multiple gifts to Indiana University spanning nearly forty years, Larry and Lucie never lost sight of their primary intent. They invested in people so people can do what people do: transform society and bring about better quality of life. That is the legacy of Larry and Lucie Glaubinger at Indiana University.

The Glaubingers understand the power of education to transform lives and bring great benefits to society.

Curt Simic
President Emeritus,
Indiana University Foundation

Photo: Kelley School of Business,
Indiana University

ED KELLEY

The Gift of a Name

Well-established and highly respected commercial names echoed throughout the life of Estel Wood (Ed) Kelley, a Class of 1939 graduate of Indiana University.

When Ed died in 2003, his obituary in the *New York Times* noted the brands and names that represented milestones of achievement and influence in his lifelong entrepreneurial career: Standard Brands, R. H. Macy, General Foods, Heublein, Consolidated Cigar, Gulf & Western, and Fairmont Foods.

During his leadership at General Foods and Fairmont Foods, the *Times* noted, Ed helped develop or introduce big-name products like Tang, Cool Whip, Grey Poupon, Smirnoff vodka, Klondike ice cream bars, and A1 Steak Sauce. And in 1981, his investment group, Kelley & Partners Ltd., purchased a company called Steak 'n Shake that was destined to become famous for its sit-down service, steak burgers, and hand-dipped milkshakes.

Given his success with some of the best-known food names and brands in the United States, Ed Kelley no doubt clearly understood the significance of a conversation he had in 1997 with Myles Brand, president of Indiana University, and Dan Dalton, dean of the IU School of Business. The three discussed the importance of named schools in the world of business, specifically, how a name on a school offered a distinctive competitive branding advantage.

Ed had just structured a major gift to fund a new undergraduate scholarship initiative at the IU School of Business that was to be patterned after the university's prestigious Wells Scholars program. President

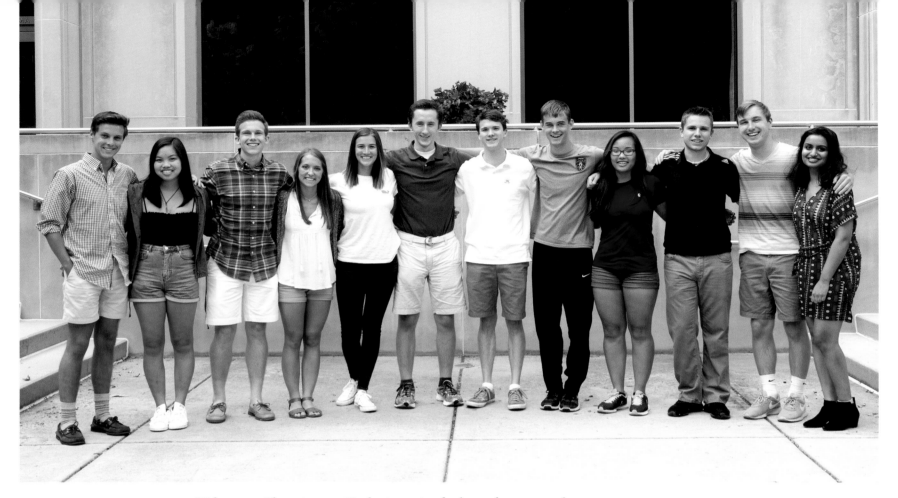

Welcome to Bloomington. Twelve incoming freshmen from across the Hoosier state gather upon arrival at IU Bloomington to celebrate their naming as Kelley Scholars. From left are Evan Castle, Caroline Chang, Mick Thompson, Mary Barnard, Hannah Bauner, William Marxer, Nick Broderick, Ethan Worrall, Lily Rexing, Colin McMonagle, Jackson Holforty, and Abi Ghiridharan. *Photo: Kelley School of Business, Indiana University*

Brand proposed that, in honor of the gift, the business school be renamed in Ed's honor, thus becoming the university's first named school.

> *Herman Wells was fond of saying that IU's alumni are among its greatest treasures because they have a sense of the past and a vision for the future. Ed Kelley's life and his relationship with the university exemplify that sentiment in the best ways possible.*
>
> *Gerald L. Bepko*
> *Interim President, Indiana University*

AN INDIANA UPBRINGING

Born in Sharpsville, Indiana, about six miles south of Kokomo, Ed grew up on a family farm and never lost his interest in foods. He grew food, he managed food, he helped create new foods, he invested in food, and he served food.

Ed was a farmer, "and, often times, he was most comfortable dressed like a farmer," Alan B. Gilman, a fellow alumnus who served with Ed on several Indiana University boards and advisory groups, says. Ed's love for growing food—particularly growing large, beautiful tomatoes—was a lifelong one, according to Alan. In the Indiana summertime, Ed would harvest tomatoes from his personal garden and would visit Steak 'n Shake restaurants around Kokomo—dressed, of course, in his bib overalls—and give tomatoes to restaurant staff and customers.

Ed kept the family farm throughout his life, eventually transforming it into the Kelley Historical Agricultural Museum that sits today along US 31 south of Kokomo. His Hoosier roots and a philosophy of giving back "what society helped me get" led to a lifelong commitment of generosity and service both to higher education and to the Kokomo community.

Part of that giving back for the Kelley family was to endow the directorship of the IU Eskenazi Museum of Art. Ed's wife, Wilma, made a planned gift to originate the endowment, and, today, the director holds the title of Wilma E. Kelley Director.

Elected to the Kelley School of Business Academy of Alumni Fellows, Ed was a member of the Indiana University Foundation Board of Directors for thirty years. He was recognized by IU with its Distinguished Alumni Service Award and, in 1971, an honorary degree.

> *Leadership and commitment endure in many forms. There is no greater expression of either, however, than by example. Mr. Kelley has impeccable credentials as a leader in corporate and entrepreneurship America.*
>
> *Dan Dalton*
> *Dean, Kelley School of Business*

Ed Kelley did not set out to name a business school when he made a major gift to his alma mater in the late 1990s. His philanthropy had long supported IU, and, many years earlier, in 1969, he had established the first fully funded professorship and chair in the IU School of Business.

His business associate, Alan Gilman, said that Ed's philanthropy was focused on offering greater opportunity to business undergraduates. "Ed wanted to enable the business school to attract the best and the brightest in the same way the Wells Scholars program was accomplishing for the College of Arts and Sciences at Indiana University," Alan said.

Alan, who was leading Steak 'n Shake at the time, said he and Ed had frequently talked about how the university was helping create the next generation of leaders in academe through the Wells Scholars program. "Ed dreamed of creating something similar for students in business. His dream was for the IU School of Business to become the number one undergraduate program in the US," Alan said.

"Ed's entire point of focus was undergraduates," Alan said. "He was thinking of kids in Indiana and nearby states who may have been the first in their families to attend college and who wanted a business school education in their home state."

Ed's gift—one of the largest in the history of Indiana University at the time—funded the Kelley Scholars, which each year awards exceptionally qualified incoming freshman students from Indiana with four consecutive years of tuition and fees, a living expenses stipend, and opportunity for study abroad. The students must commit to academic excellence, achieve a minimum GPA of 3.5, and be a part of the Business Honors Program.

"WHY DON'T WE DO SOMETHING ABOUT IT?"

Ed Kelley spoke directly and asked good questions that frequently prompted action at his alma mater, according to Curt Simic, president emeritus of the Indiana University Foundation.

Curt recalls a presentation he made once to the Indiana University Foundation Board of Directors when Ed Kelley was at the table. "We were talking about how IU lagged in the number of endowed chairs and how this deficit was harmful to the overall positioning of the university," Curt says.

The painful fact was that IU was close to the bottom of the Big Ten in overall endowed chairs and professorships.

Far from just a point of pride, the number of endowed chairs and professorships at a major research university often has a direct influence on its ability to recruit outstanding faculty. Schools with endowed chairs can offer both greater security and higher compensation packages to attract exceptional faculty.

Ed, according to Curt, listened carefully to the presentation that day at the IU Foundation and then

"Mr. Kelley, a modest man, did not request that the School of Business be named in his honor," Dan Dalton, former dean of the Kelley School of Business, said. "In fact, he had no interest in such recognition. He only agreed to be so honored because he knew that it was important for the School of Business and for Indiana University."

Ed Kelley had a longstanding passion for the undergraduate program in business at IU, Dan said. And the passion did not end with the major gift he made. Year after year afterward, Ed would attend the annual dinner to welcome the entering class of Kelley Scholars to the Bloomington campus.

"At every one of those dinners, Mr. Kelley would be overwhelmed, and he often cried with joy. He was so happy to see the newest class entering the Kelley School. He loved these students and treated them as if they were his own kids," Dan said.

Dan Dalton visited Ed regularly at his downtown Indianapolis office, and the two, of course, often ate lunch at Steak 'n Shake. "Mr. Kelley would never accept my money to pay for lunch, nor the university's or the school's money," Dan explained.

In addition to funding the Kelley Scholars program, Ed supported the Virgil T. DeVault Alumni Center, the Indiana University Jacobs School of Music, the John Mellencamp Pavilion, and the Alva Prickett Chair in Accounting on the Bloomington campus. At IU Kokomo, his generosity funded several student scholarships and three buildings.

"Indiana University and the Kelley School of Business have never had a better friend," Dan said.

asked, "Why don't we do something about it?" He paused and then added, "We've been hearing about this for years now. What are we going to do about it?"

And in a moment, Curt said, he realized that the board had just been challenged by one of its senior, most highly respected members to take on the most substantial task it would accomplish during Curt's tenure as president of the IU Foundation.

"When Ed asked that hard question, I thought to myself, 'We're going to make this work,'" Curt said.

The result of Ed's question and the determination by the IU Foundation board to address one of the university's most critical needs—endowed chairs and endowed professorships—was the Indiana University Endowment Campaign launched in 1994 with a preliminary goal of $350 million.

Ed Kelley

The campaign was dramatically successful, moving Indiana University from the bottom to the top of the Big Ten in the total number of endowed chairs and professorships.

The Endowment Campaign concluded with more than 150,000 donors giving a total of $504,302,229, more than 144 percent of the campaign goal. The campaign not only generated new faculty positions but then, in turn, enabled IU to compete more effectively for exceptionally talented students, as well. "Endowments ensure a continual increase in the number of new undergraduate scholarships and graduate fellowships that the campus can award annually," Curt said.

Academic distinction is not built in a year or two. It requires long-term investments and commitments by key leaders inside and outside the university. In this sense, endowments are very much an insurance policy for continued excellence.

Curt Simic
President Emeritus,
Indiana University Foundation

"The intentional effort that was realized through the successful Endowment Campaign was, without a doubt, the greatest focused fundraising success we had at Indiana University during my time there," Curt said.

"Not only did we determine to address IU's most critical need, but President Myles Brand also devised a strategy to be able to match the income from gifts given to the campaign," he added.

"This matching component of the campaign effectively doubled the value of each gift and created a scenario for success so the university finished the campaign in a much more competitive position," Curt said.

"And it was, in many ways, a profound answer to Ed Kelley's hard question," Curt concluded.

THE STANDING OVATION

There was one tribute paid to Ed Kelley when he died in 2003 that, most likely, would have pleased him immensely.

Dan Dalton, dean of the Kelley School of Business at the time, remembers the memorial service held at the Columbia Club, on Monument Circle in down-town Indianapolis. Family members, friends, and business colleagues had gathered to honor Ed. The club was filled absolutely to capacity, Dan recalls.

Just before the formal program began, the single door at the back of the room opened and forty or fifty young students entered.

"These students—all Indiana University Kelley Scholars who were dressed to the nines—walked in and stood side by side against the far wall, as all seats were taken," Dan said. "They remained there for the entire ceremony and left as one when the program concluded," he added.

To this day, Dan does not know who orchestrated the remarkable assembly of Kelley Scholars to pay tribute to the individual who had made their educational experience at Indiana University possible. "It was not me," he says. "But I know how absolutely elated Ed Kelley would have been with such a standing ovation from his Kelley Scholars."

*Photo: Indiana University
Foundation*

MARY MARGARET WEBB

To Help Others Do What They Love

Adventure. Fun. Motherhood. Four university degrees in four different decades. Fun, fun, fun. And twenty-six charitable gift annuities in fourteen years.

That's twenty-six gifts so doctoral students in the Indiana University School of Education receive essential training to influence young lives for generations to come.

As told by the one who lived it, the story of Mary Margaret Webb, a 1983 Indiana University PhD alumna, is extraordinary and humorous. And it's punctuated with story after story of a noteworthy enthusiasm and exhilaration for life.

It's a story about growing up in Johnson County, marrying the love of her life at the age of 18, and having three youngsters before she started college. And it's a story about a lifelong commitment to elementary school teaching, a most-loved career that provided her the challenge, the success, and the fun to "keep life interesting."

THREE KIDS, THEN COLLEGE

Born in Crawford County, Indiana, Mary Margaret was the eldest of five children. Her family farmed in Johnson County so she learned the essential daily tasks: driving tractors, planting seed, milking cows. And, she proudly boasts, she "could still throw bales on a flatbed" at the age of twenty-five.

Mary Margaret waited to start college until her hands, literally, were quite full. But her three children—ages two, three, and five—were not about to become obstacles to doing something she had dreamed about since she was seven years old.

Connect, Collaborate, Create. A state-of-the-art technology workspace in the Indiana University School of Education, C3@Education encourages group collaboration and provides small spaces for student and faculty work teams. Integrating technology into the teaching profession is a school-wide emphasis and culminates in the Instructional Systems Technology Fellowships established by Mary Margaret Webb for IU graduate students. *Photo: James Brosher, Indiana University Communications*

"In second grade, I absolutely loved my teacher, because she made school so much fun and so interesting. She helped me decide—right then and there—that I too was going to be a teacher when I grew up," Mary Margaret said.

And that's exactly what she became.

She enrolled at nearby Franklin College full-time and graduated, cum laude, in just three and a half years. Who took care of the babies? "No problem. I either got a babysitter or took them to my mom's. If I couldn't find anybody else, I took them with me to class," she said.

Took three babies to a college history class? "Yes, I put them in the back of the classroom with crayons and coloring books," she explained. "And I told them: 'You are to sit here, and you are to be quiet. Not get up and run around. It'll just be an hour. Then, we'll go do something special.'"

That was only the beginning for this teacher and elementary school principal. In fact, it was the first of her four college degrees earned in four different decades. In 1959, it was the bachelor's degree at Franklin College. In 1964, it was an elementary education master's degree at Butler University in Indianapolis, followed by the Indiana University specialist degree in elementary reading education in 1979. Finally, she earned her PhD in school administration, also at IU, in 1983.

To Mary Margaret, teaching was a dream career, plain and simple. The stories this IU alumna tells about her teaching days are inspiring and, frankly, fun.

When she was a half-time principal and half-time classroom teacher the last eight years of her career, one of her students was having difficulty with regular attendance. "I said to him, 'Jimmy, if you don't come to school tomorrow, I'm going to come and get you.'"

And she did. She left school and drove to her young student's home. When Jimmy's mother came to the door, Mary Margaret said, "Tell Jimmy to get dressed. We're going to school."

"I waited, and Jimmy got dressed. I got him in my car and fastened his seat belt, and we went to school." Never, the story concludes, did Jimmy fail to come to school again.

With great pride and a deep sense of fulfillment, Mary Margaret will show you the quilt she keeps in her living room now. It was a gift upon her retirement from Franklin Community Schools and includes tribute after tribute from her colleagues and former students. One of the panels reads, "To one of my favorite teachers: she expected a lot from her students and her students responded. She is definitely one of the reasons I became a teacher. Thank you, Dr. Webb."

Such tributes are common occurrences in Mary Margaret's life. She was honored by her first alma mater, Franklin College, with its Distinguished Alumni Award in 2016. But more significant to her are the individuals she meets whenever she is out and about in Franklin. She loves meeting former students who stop her and thank her for the lessons taught in her classrooms. "It's so much fun to see them now and learn how their lives have progressed," she says.

SUSTAINING TOMORROW'S TEACHERS

Mary Margaret Webb's desire to help others experience the satisfaction of doing what they love is one reason she and her late husband, Denzil, became philanthropists, according to John Keith, JD, formerly associate vice president of individual giving at the Indiana University Foundation and now a consultant at Johnson Grossnickle Associates.

"Mary Margaret and Denzil cared very deeply for education, both higher ed and K–12," John said. In addition to their gifts to Indiana University, the Webbs funded scholarships and fellowships at Franklin College, the University of Indianapolis, and Butler University.

Mary Margaret is very specific about why she has chosen to philanthropically support the next generation of school teachers and administrators. "Teaching in the public schools wasn't a job, it was a calling for me," Mary Margaret said. "The kids I taught in school are now in their sixties," she explained. "And many of them became teachers too. I hear from them regularly and always love to learn about their careers, about their lives, about their own kids."

When Mary Margaret and Denzil first began giving to higher education, they had received an invitation to help fund a new campus building at one of her alma maters. "Buildings get burned down," the two concluded. "We wanted to invest in people. We started that a long time ago and have always dedicated our giving to scholarships. Teachers of tomorrow need money to learn today," Mary Margaret said.

"Giving has been fun for both of us," Mary Margaret says of the annuities she has established. "Denzil loved giving too, and once he found out that a university is a good place to invest in people, he enjoyed it too," Mary Margaret said.

ACCESS TO GRADUATE EDUCATION

At IU Bloomington, Mary Margaret established three fellowships in the School of Education to fund graduate education for future teachers and school administrators: the School Administration Fellowship, the Instructional Systems Technology Fellowship, and the Reading Education Fellowship. All three were created to provide access to higher education long into the future for Indiana University graduate students.

A charitable gift annuity is a gift that falls into what is called planned giving in the nonprofit sector. Such gifts generally go to work in the future, upon the do-

"There is, almost always, a deep hope that motivates acts of philanthropy in higher education." Those hopes, according to Curt Simic, president emeritus of the Indiana University Foundation, are focused for many donors on "dreams that scholarship recipients will eventually make contributions to benefit community and humanity."

Commonly, Curt explained, scholarships encourage merit and are awarded to those who have already achieved and now demonstrate the potential for further achievement. "This concept of rewarding merit is one of the trademarks of higher education financial aid programs in America," Curt said. In fact, it underwrites the entire concept of the National Merit Scholarship in this country.

"It is very critical for development officers to listen," Curt said, to learn what potential benefactors hope to achieve through their giving. "The most effective partner-ships in philanthropy are borne out of clearly recognizing the donor's objective and matching it with an institutional priority," he added.

Likewise, the least effective partnerships—if partnership even develops in such situations—occur when the institution, repeatedly, tells the donor what it wants. Without hearing the donor's aspirations for giving, this kind of one-way conversation is not only ineffective, Curt said, but also disrespectful.

"Listening—truly hearing what donors want to accomplish—is the most important skill a major gifts team can possess and practice," Curt concluded.

nor's demise. But because Mary Margaret's gifts were matched during special fundraising campaigns at Indiana University, she recently had the opportunity to hear about the students who, for the first time, received graduate fellowships named in her honor.

Janet Yin-Chan Liao is a PhD candidate in instructional systems technology and helpline manager in the Office of Teacher Education. Janet's research fo-

cuses on teacher professional development for technology integration, and she has served as a technology coach in the school during her time at IU.

The Instructional Systems Technology Fellowship will enable Janet to be more effective in both data collection and analysis for her dissertation: "I will be able to visit teachers in their classrooms more frequently to provide modeling and in-class support. I'll also be

University development officers can foster exceptionally broad understandings of what matters most to donors. Because these representatives listen to donors talk about their passions, about their personal experiences, and about what they hope to accomplish through their philanthropy, there's a natural camaraderie that often flourishes between donors and development officers.

Jonathan Purvis was formerly vice president for development, regional campuses, at the Indiana University Foundation and is now vice president for advancement at Butler University. He first met Mary Margaret Webb in 2012 when he became director of development for the Indiana University School of Education in Bloomington and called one day to request an appointment with her.

His experience with Mary Margaret included assisting her in establishing five charitable gift annuities.

"Mary Margaret's deep commitment to help others is perfectly manifested in her own education career which spanned four decades. So, it's only natural that this commitment would manifest itself through her philanthropy," Jonathan said.

He explained that Mary Margaret's generosity reaches many institutions but is primarily focused on education. "She gives back through significant scholarship and fellowship support to all the institutions from which she earned degrees," Jonathan said.

Mary Margaret was also the prime mover behind the successful effort to renovate a one-room school house in Franklin, Indiana,

so local elementary school students would have a hands-on learning experience.

"It's always been clear to me that Mary Margaret Webb understood from an early age that education was the key to a better life for herself and others. But beyond that practical understanding, education became her great personal passion which permeated all aspects of her life, including her philanthropy," Jonathan said.

He added, "This great passion for education immeasurably benefitted the countless students in her classrooms over four decades. And now it continues to reach countless more who benefit from the fellowships and scholarships she established in higher education."

able to explore many different applications and teaching materials so I can offer the best recommendations to integrate technology into elementary school classrooms."

And what does Janet offer to Mary Margaret? "Thank you, Dr. Webb! Your generosity makes a difference in educational research and practice," she said.

Michael Karlin, also a PhD student in instructional systems technology, commented on how the Webb fellowship will affect his life: "In short, this fellowship will make an enormous positive difference in the amount of time and energy I am able to devote to supporting teachers."

A Commitment to Opportunity

Mary Margaret and Denzil Webb lived fully—that is clear when you hear her talk about their lives together. "One day Denzil told me that he'd like to get an airplane and learn to fly," she said.

"Let's go for it," she told him. "I like flying!"

So they bought a plane, and Denzil became a licensed pilot. Mary Margaret took lessons to become his co-pilot. One day, the Webbs were flying into a small airport and Denzil told Mary Margaret, "You're going to land this plane." Her response? "Okay!"

"I thought to myself, well, if I screw up, he'll take the controls because he's not going to crash. It took me three approaches because I had to come around a Learjet, but I thought that by the third time, I had it all lined up."

Mary Margaret landed the plane and remembers thinking, Boy, I'm better than I thought I was. "Fun," she said. "That was fun!"

Nearly every time I met Mary Margaret for lunch in Franklin, people would come up to her, identify themselves as former students, and then quickly add how much influence Mary Margaret had on their lives. Everyone—everyone—in Franklin, Indiana, knows Mary Margaret Webb.

John Keith, JD
Consultant, Johnson Grossnickle Associates; Former Associate Vice President, Individual Giving, Indiana University Foundation

Is there much else on the bucket list for Mary Margaret? "Yes, there is," this eighty-seven-year-old will tell you. "I want to jump out of an airplane . . . with somebody holding on to me, of course. It's been on the list for some time," she said.

"By the way," she added, "I'm not done giving yet."

She paused and then said, "I have a meeting coming up soon with the IU School of Education to talk about the next annuities I want to give. This time, I want to give them in my daughter's name."

If one were to select a song describing Mary Margaret Webb's life, Frank Sinatra's "My Way" would be a perfect fit.

Franklin College Announcement of Mary Margaret Webb as Recipient of the 2016 Distinguished Alumni Award

Note: Mary Margaret Webb died January 11, 2018, in Franklin, Indiana.

A Commitment to Distinction

STIMULATING CREATIVITY
AND EXCELLENCE AT
INDIANA UNIVERSITY

Giving to higher education continues to increase in the United States, according to *Giving USA 2017: The Annual Report on Philanthropy for the Year 2016,* researched and written by the Indiana University Lilly Family School of Philanthropy.

Private giving across the United States to all educational institutions, which totaled $59.77 billion in 2016, is often the difference between just keeping the doors open and the achievement of excellence.

At Indiana University, private donors have consistently chosen to support programs and endeavors that are, at times, both founded and nurtured through philanthropy. A new academic center might begin with a faculty member's gift. An art museum may be remodeled and positioned for distinction. Schools and colleges may perhaps receive the funding so essential to maturation and realization of their original vision.

Indiana University has, most fortunately, achieved distinction through the generosity of its most loyal alumni and friends.

Photo: Indiana University Foundation

SIDNEY & LOIS ESKENAZI

Lessons in Philanthropy

Sidney Eskenazi learned his first lessons of giving early in life.

When Sid was young, his father had a wholesale produce business at the corner of South and New Jersey streets in downtown Indianapolis. There was no refrigeration, so his dad would bring leftover vegetables and fruit home for dinner each night. And every so often, two women—"dressed something like penguins with their long black dresses and huge white hats"—would come by and Sid's dad would fill large bags with food for them. The women were from a religious order, the Little Sisters of the Poor, and they would take the food to feed those in need.

"When my father brought home the vegetables each day from the market, one of us would go to neighbors and ask if they could use some peas or green beans or some lettuce or onions," Sid explained. "Whatever we had, we had to share with people."

BUILDING COMMUNITY

Community resources were important to Sid as a kid growing up in Indianapolis. In his neighborhood, the Jewish Community Center offered a gym, ping-pong, billiards, painting classes, and books and magazines for reading. "I've always been grateful for a place like that to go. They took care of us," Sid recalls, "and it kept us off the streets and out of trouble."

Early life experiences often prompt both fond memories and new advocacy as benefactors take action to make a difference with their philanthropy in their own communities. With Sid, the significance of a community resource like the one he experienced as

a child was prominent in his mind when he and his wife, Lois, were asked to consider a gift for an aquatic center at the new Jewish Community Center on the north side of Indianapolis. "That's something I knew I'd be very interested in doing," he said. "I really enjoyed seeing that water park come about."

Sid recalled other memories of life in Indianapolis during his childhood. When people in his neighborhood were ill, and could not afford health care on their own, they were taken to the old City Hospital. The hospital was opened to treat the smallpox epidemic in 1859 and was the primary health-care provider for the city's indigent. Since the 1908 founding of the IU School of Medicine in Indianapolis, City Hospital has served as one of the teaching sites for medical school residents in the city.

City Hospital was renamed Indianapolis General Hospital in 1947 and renamed again in 1975 as Wishard Memorial Hospital. In 2009, a referendum to build a new Wishard Hospital campus was approved with support from over 85 percent of the voters.

Enter Lois and Sid, again in a community building initiative. After the referendum, the fundraising staff from Wishard contacted Sid and requested permission to bring him a major gift proposal.

"I knew that we wanted to help with the construction of the new hospital because I love Indianapolis, and I wanted to do some good for my community here," Sid recalls. "We thought we might donate a room or something like that."

But the proposal ignited Sid's enthusiasm—so much so that he remembers calling Lois at home after his meeting with the Wishard representatives and telling her about the opportunity.

"I felt it was the right thing to do," Sid recalls. "Here's a chance to really impact the lives of a lot of people," he said, "and it had a link to IU through the School of Medicine. To me, this was an opportunity to give my kids and grandkids an inheritance that would go on forever."

Lois and Sid discussed the proposal, and Sid determined, "I want to do it. This is really what I would like to be my life's legacy."

In 2011, the gift that resulted in the renaming of the new facility was announced, and the Sidney and Lois Eskenazi Hospital and Eskenazi Health campus opened in downtown Indianapolis in 2013.

THE GUARDIAN ANGEL

Sid was born in Indianapolis in 1930 and grew up in the south side Sephardic Jewish community. When his father died in 1944, Sid's uncle became what Sid called "the greatest person in my life because I had no father."

The uncle, Naphtali Eskenazi, was firm in his insistence that Sid pursue college after high school. But Sid, who was "making a quarter an hour in my work, and sometimes, if I worked weekends, I got fifty cents an hour," resisted.

Facing
The Space to Show.
The galleries in Eskenazi Hall offer more than six thousand square feet of combined exhibition space for the Herron School of Art and Design to showcase artwork of both emerging and established artists. "Deep in the Shallows," an exhibition by Michael Zansky, featured sixteen- by twelve-foot carved plywood paintings and a series of burnt drawings on paper for a show in early 2018.
Photo: Jake Sneath, Herron School of Art and Design, Indiana University

THE VALUE OF A NAME

"They said what I had been thinking about for a long, long time."

That was Sid Eskenazi's reaction to reading about two American philanthropists, Woody Hunt and Orville Rogers, and their decisions to attach their names publicly to their giving.

Woody Hunt, then chairman and CEO of Hunt Companies, Inc., told the story that for many years the giving he and his wife achieved through their family foundation was done anonymously because the couple did not want public recognition.

"We changed that because at several fundraising events, people who were soliciting us convinced me that the way to do the most good was to be recognized. In so doing, you set standards for others that (can be used) to solicit others, and it creates peer pressure," Hunt explained.

Orville Rogers, a retired airline pilot turned philanthropist, agreed, saying "I'm willing to let my giving be known to people who might be interested, in the hopes that it might inspire them to do good works themselves."

Sid agreed with the philanthropists. "If you lend your name to a project, it encourages others to say, 'Well, if he can do something like that, perhaps I can do something too.'"

"By linking our names to initiatives or letting our names be put on a building, for example, Lois and I hope that others may find inspiration to take action for similar good," Sid said. "That's part of the cycle that you hope to begin by giving in the first place."

"That was some pretty good money for a kid in those days. Why did I have to go to school?" he asked. But Uncle Naphtali—who Sid now calls "his guardian angel"—insisted and told Sid, "If you go to IU, I'll help pay for it."

Sid enrolled at IU and never forgot his uncle's influence and inspiration. Years later, when Eskenazi Health opened, the small, nondenominational chapel in the new facility was named in honor of Uncle Naphtali.

After graduating with a degree in accounting in 1950, Sid went on to law school, another move that Uncle Naphtali encouraged, and received his IU law degree in 1953. He and Lois Cohen were married in 1954.

FIRST GIFTS

As a young attorney in Indianapolis, Sid went to work for a start-up real estate developer in the city. And soon he was in a position to give his first gift to Indiana University. The story behind that gift is one that Sid still likes to tell today.

School was never easy for Sid Eskenazi, but he didn't realize until he was an adult that he had a learning disability that made it difficult for him to retain information he had read. "I did the work, I read the material, I went to class every day. But I could not remember what I had read," he says.

His reading challenges prompted Sid to leave Bloomington and continue his studies in Indianapolis, so he could focus more and complete his law degree.

It wasn't long into his work as a corporate attorney that the real estate development company produced "a little windfall," prompting Sid to consider his first gift to his alma mater. And there was no doubt about his intention: "I wanted to provide scholarships for C students in the IU Law School," Sid said, "because there was no money for C students. All the money went to the A students."

"Those are the kids who needed help—the kids who only got Cs," Sid says. So he contacted Indiana University and established a scholarship fund for law school students both on the Bloomington and Indianapolis campuses. Since then, the Eskenazi scholarship fund has provided well over a hundred scholarships for IU law school students.

Through the years, the C average has been changed as a requirement for the Eskenazi scholarships because of different expectations for students to maintain higher grade point averages in law school. But still today, Sid knows that he's building another form of legacy through the scholarship endowment. "I want these students to know that someone came in here and helped them. I expect, at some point in their lives, they will remember that and help somebody else," he says.

THE LOVE OF ART

In his early days as a private practice attorney, Sid had an experience that sparked his interest and led to a lifelong passion for works of art.

"I met a clothing company salesman in Indianapolis who wanted to open a clothing store. He needed legal work done, and I was happy to have a client," Sid says.

But when Sid gave the businessman an invoice for his legal services, the owner said, "I can't pay you. I'm broke."

"I have to get paid," Sid responded. "I have a family, I have an office, and I need to get paid. You must have something."

"Yeah, I do have one thing. I bought this Joan Miró signed lithograph when things were good for me," the business owner told Sid.

"I'll take it," Sid said.

"I hung the Miró lithograph in our home, and it made a strong impression on me. I'd walk by it and look at it, and I liked the way it looked. There's something about images like this that makes you feel good," Sid says.

The Miró lithograph began a lifetime of art collection for Sid and Lois. Eventually, they collected thirty-four Miró etchings, lithographs, and drawings from late in the Spanish master's career. The Eskenazi art collection also included prints by Marc Chagall, Alexander Calder, Pablo Picasso, Sam Francis, Tom Wesselmann, Jean Dubuffet, Salvador Dali, and Pierre-Auguste Renoir.

Following the practice they set in motion with the Jewish Community Center gift, the Eskenazis made a lead gift to the Indiana University Museum of Art in

"I represented a man who was older—in his nineties—and who had quite a bit of money. I encouraged him to give some of the money away but had a terrible time getting him to do it," Sid Eskenazi says of one of his law practice clients.

"I had an IU Foundation representative I was working with, and I asked him to find something that would interest my client," Sid explained. Sid and the development officer, Phillip K. Hardwick, took the client to different IU locations, entertained him, and showed him places and programs that would benefit from his generosity. But nothing struck the gentleman's fancy.

Finally, Phil, who was vice president for Indiana University Purdue University Indianapolis (IUPUI) development at the Indiana University Foundation, said to Sid, "For thirty years, we've been trying to get a lead gift to fund a new Herron

School of Art facility on the IUPUI campus. We're scattered in a few buildings at Sixteenth and Pennsylvania streets in Indianapolis and are all over the place. We need a new facility badly."

Sid replied, "Forget him. That's something my wife and I would be interested in. Let's work it out."

So they did.

The home of the Herron School of Art and Design on the IUPUI campus is now Sidney and Lois Eskenazi Hall and houses art and design studios, five galleries, an internationally recognized art library, student exhibition spaces, and the Grand Hall for public receptions and events.

The Eskenazi gift in 2000 was part of Herron's first-ever capital campaign and enabled the school's long-hoped-for move to the IUPUI campus from a downtown Indianapolis neighborhood.

2016 that included cash and their collection of nearly one hundred works of art by twentieth-century European and American masters. The gift was designated for the renovation of the museum's I. M. Pei building, which originally opened in 1982.

With this gift we are combining two of our greatest passions: Indiana University and art. We are delighted that our collection, which we have loved building and living with, will find a home at the museum.

Sid and Lois Eskenazi
May 11, 2016

PASSING THE CRAFT ON

How does a philanthropist pass on his craft to the next generation?

Mostly by living the example of giving.

In 2016, Sid and Lois's children, David, Sandra, and Dori, made a gift in honor of their parents to the Indiana University School of Medicine to establish an endowed fund for a new distinguished cancer researcher.

Lois had been diagnosed with lung cancer several years earlier and was treated by IU oncologist Lawrence Einhorn, MD. "At the initial diagnosis, the results weren't good, but we were very lucky and it was operable," David Eskenazi said.

David continued, "I understand that's not the case for everybody. But it's always getting better because of people like Dr. Einhorn, the individuals he works with at the IU School of Medicine, and the research they do. Year after year they're making cancer more treatable and curable. My sisters and I are honored to be able to do something to recognize that."

In 2014, following in her parents' footsteps, Sandra Eskenazi made new technology accessible to burn patients at Eskenazi Health with her gift to fund an innovative laser therapy treatment option—one of only three such treatment capabilities in the country. She also gave the lead gift to construct the Sandra Eskenazi Center for Brain Care Innovation for patients with Alzheimer's and other forms of dementia.

In the Eskenazi family, the giving is surely to continue into the next-next generation.

"Every month you see me," Sid Eskenazi told his grandchildren one day, "I'm going to give you a twenty dollar bill. That's five dollars a week, and here's what's going to happen. With four dollars, you can do anything you want each week: buy gum, get an ice cream, or do whatever you want. But one dollar of the five must go to charity. Put it in the boxes at the grocery store or take it to your Sunday school. I don't care what you do, as long as it goes to charity."

When Sid next sees his grandkids, he asks them, "Did you give your money to charity?"

"Yup," come the answers.

"All right then, here's your next twenty dollar bill."

Sid had started, undoubtedly without the intention of doing so, a small ripple among his friends and asso-ciates. Curt Simic, president emeritus of the Indiana University Foundation, was among those who began to follow the practice.

"After Sid told me about teaching his grandchildren to be aware of the needs of others, I decided to give our own grandkids the same opportunity," Curt said. "I gave each twenty-five dollars, told them that half of it had to be given to a charity, and asked them to let me know how they spent it," Curt said.

"As children of the technology age, the kids made a video to report back to me," Curt explained. "I watched the video and learned that they had not kept any of the gift for themselves, because while they were researching the charities, they found that the need was much greater than they originally thought. And they determined that they could do more than required if they gave it all away."

"I decided right then to double the gift the next year," Curt concluded.

CORPORATE—AND PERSONAL—PRIORITIES

Sandor Development is the real estate development company Sid Eskenazi founded in 1963. Today, it is one of the country's largest privately held shopping center developers, with retail space in twenty-five states. David is president of the company now, which is headquartered on the north side of Indianapolis.

Corporate websites have a way of relaying something of the priorities of the people behind a business endeavor.

The website of Sandor Development contains, of course, the usual corporate public relations statements and news releases. But intertwined, at irregular junctures, are notices that communicate a significant part of the company's culture.

Headlines like "Giving Tuesday 2016," "Sandor Employees Team Up with Habitat for Humanity," and "Sandor Helps Raise $30,000 for Gleaners Food Bank" speak volumes about the corporation that Sid Eskenazi founded more than fifty years ago in Indianapolis, the city he loved then and still loves today.

This incredibly generous gift from the Eskenazis in support of the art museum is heartening and uplifting—but it is hardly surprising. In the many years I have had the pleasure of knowing Sid and Lois, they have consistently demonstrated a deep-seated love for the students of Indiana University and an unwavering commitment to enriching the student experience on the Bloomington campus.

Lauren Robel
Provost and Executive Vice President, Indiana University Bloomington

Facing
Envisioning the New.
A skyway bridge and entrance on the north side of the building designed by I. M. Pei will enhance the Sidney and Lois Eskenazi Museum of Art after renovation. *Photo: Indiana University*

Photo: Indiana University Foundation

DAVID HENRY JACOBS

Stand and Sing

One Thursday night in the fall semester of his sophomore year at Indiana University, David Henry Jacobs went to find a choir practice at the First Methodist Church in downtown Bloomington.

"On Thursdays, pretty much all over the world, Methodist churches have choir practice," David explained.

"And I was not in a very great space in my head at this time. But I knew that when everything's wrong, we in the Methodist church stand and sing. Chaos can be descending, but you must not forget to stand and sing," he says.

That night in downtown Bloomington, David met Charles H. Webb. Charles was then associate dean of the Indiana University School of Music and also happened to be the organist at First Methodist Church.

The next year, in 1973, Charles would become dean of the School of Music.

Charles introduced himself to David and welcomed the young baritone to the choir. David recalls watching Charles play the organ during rehearsal and remembers that he had two thoughts: "I wonder if I could ever play like that" and "I think that man is going to be a friend of mine."

And so began a lifelong friendship between the dean of a world-renowned music school and a twenty-year-old would-be organ major from Cleveland, Ohio. The friendship quickly included Charles's wife, Kenda McGibbon Webb, who a few weeks later introduced herself to David and invited him to lunch at their home.

David accepted the invitation. "That was the first time I met the Webb boys—I called them three, five,

To university fundraisers, nothing means more than to follow the intention—both in deed and spirit—of a generous donor.

While "donor intent" is an abiding concept in fundraising circles, there is increasingly in nonprofits an urgent need for giving that is unrestricted. Such funding, to be used at the discretion of chief administrators, can be a critical resource to a school that is in the process of reaching new heights and experimenting with new paths of instruction and learning.

The Jacobs School of Music was such an institution in 2005. And the Jacobs family, because of its relationship with the dean of the school, knew the significance of unrestricted gifts. The family specified a portion of its major gift for funding new and, as of yet, undefined initiatives.

"A gift like this," David Henry Jacobs explained, "is based in trust and relationship. My parents trusted Charles Webb to take the school of music into the public—to take students to New York City and be the only school that's ever done that."

The gift, likewise, provided funds "so that when Leonard Bernstein wanted students from the IU music school to perform at his seventieth birthday concert at Tanglewood, the dean had the financial wherewithal to hire the buses and get the orchestra to the Berkshire Hills in western Massachusetts," David said.

"The world learns about the Jacobs School when our students perform. In Bloomington, to be sure, but also at points scattered around the world," David says. The private giving of his parents, he adds, helped make the earliest appearances of Jacobs School students possible in some of music's most acclaimed performance venues.

major benefactors, David knows this intrinsically. "This is one of the things about the Jacobs School that I know: you put the students in front of an audience and the audience is hooked, every time," he says.

The bulk of David's gift to the Bicentennial Campaign—something not new for a member of the Jacobs family—was designated for the Jacobs Family Bicentennial Scholars and Fellows in honor, naturally, of Dean Emeritus Charles H. Webb.

We have students from every state and fifty countries, and many don't come with the resources they need to really push their academic boundaries. These scholarships will enable these talented young musicians to truly drink in the educational knowledge available from our outstanding faculty.

Charles H. Webb
Dean Emeritus,
Indiana University Jacobs School of Music

David Henry Jacobs

GRATITUDE

Kari Novilla hails from Jefferson City, Tennessee, and is a sophomore Bachelor of Music in Harp Performance student at the Jacobs School of Music. She studies with Elzbieta Szmyt and is the recipient of a scholarship funded by the Jacobs family that makes her education at Indiana University possible.

Like many of those whose dreams are touched by the generosity of university donors, Kari is finding exceptional opportunities at Indiana University: "Thanks to you, Mr. Jacobs, I am here. I cried on the sidewalk outside a store in my hometown when I opened the email saying that I had received the Barbara and David Jacobs Scholarship.

"I find it extraordinary that all in one place I can cultivate my love of music, develop lifelong friendships, and work on myself as a human being—all in hopes of bringing about a better tomorrow.

"Thank you ever so much for this once-in-a-lifetime opportunity that I will never take for granted. It is people like you who help dreams come true and give me joy in pursuit of my happiness: music."

In addition to his generosity to the school that bears his family name, David supports the Indiana University Lilly Family School of Philanthropy, the Maurer School of Law, the Kinsey Institute, the Eskenazi Museum of Art, and the LGBTQ+ Alumni Association.

And following in his mother's tradition, David has been a member of the Indiana University Foundation Board of Directors since 2006. He is a founding member of the Women's Philanthropy Leadership Council of the IU Foundation.

Melissa Korzec Dickson, executive director of external affairs at the Jacobs School of Music, explains what she calls a defining characteristic of David as a philanthropist. "It's uncommon for a donor to show both the passion for and the understanding of a school's mission to the extent that David does," she says.

Melissa explained that when she, Dean Gwyn Richards, and David were discussing his most recent gift to the Jacobs School of Music, David asked one simple question, "What is it that you need?"

"He's most concerned about what the school requires to achieve its potential and to help students achieve their promise," Melissa said. "His spirit of generosity is demonstrated in that simple question that David asks so very often: 'What is it that you need?'"

Is it puzzling that this leadership and loyalty come from someone who left Indiana University as a student?

David says not. "Some might find it ironic that for the past five decades, I've nurtured a passionate loyalty for a school that I voluntarily chose to leave," he explained.

"Yet it has always made perfect sense to me because my time at IU was probably the most valuable in my life. This is because of the wisdom, the patience, and the vision of one couple, Dean Charles Webb and his open-hearted and embracing wife, Kenda Webb," David said.

> *Our relationship with David is, by far, his greatest gift to us. Beyond his extraordinary generosity, David is truly an inspiration through his leadership, passion, and partnership with the school. He is not simply a friend, patron, advocate, or advisor of this great university, but an active partner—participating with us each day in moving us toward the aspirations we hold.*
>
> *Gwyn Richards*
> *David Henry Jacobs Bicentennial Dean,*
> *Jacobs School of Music*

David is quick to credit his parents' role in modeling giving as an abiding influence in his life. "My parents were amazingly generous people. They both did so many wonderful things, unheralded, for so many people and organizations," David said.

He stops, reflects, and then adds, "If, in my lifetime, I could be one-tenth of what they became, I'd be tap dancing on air."

> *I hope that my mother's gift will ensure that the excellence for which the Jacobs School is known will continue long into the future. Nothing would be more gratifying to me than to know that talented and deserving young musicians will be able to pursue a superb musical education because my mother cared.*
>
> *David Henry Jacobs*

Photo: Indiana University Foundation

ELINOR OSTROM

Steadfast Loyalty

Being named one of the world's most influential people by *Time* was an honor that came to Indiana University Distinguished Professor Elinor (Lin) Ostrom in the last year of her life. The magazine noted in its April 18, 2012 issue, "After the TARP bailouts and the devastation of democracies in Europe by financial technocrats, the world is again beginning to appreciate what Elinor Ostrom has deeply, persistently and quietly been illuminating for nearly fifty years."

The *Time* accolade was quite an honor, by any measure. But it no doubt paled when set alongside the Nobel Prize in Economic Sciences Lin had received three years earlier.

How does a woman who was advised against a PhD program in economics—because she was a woman—attain a Nobel Prize in economics? How does she, at the age of seventy-eight, attain rank on a list of the world's most influential?

Most likely by learning, as she put it, "not to take initial rejections as permanent obstacles to moving ahead." And by demonstrating persistence, deep commitment, and quiet determination.

This is a day that started with a big surprise. Your phone rings at six thirty in the morning and you wonder if that is someone calling with a recording. I was very surprised that there was a real human at the other end, indicating that the call was from Stockholm and that the [Nobel] committee had made its decision. What a way to start a Monday morning!

Elinor Ostrom
October 12, 2009

Officially, Lin won the Sveriges Riksbank Prize in Economic Sciences in Memory of Alfred Nobel 2009 "for her analysis of economic governance, especially the commons." She shared the prize with Oliver E. Williamson from the University of California, Berkeley.

Analysis of economic governance was a lifetime work for Lin and was founded on hundreds of studies of fish stocks, pastures, woods, lakes, and groundwater basins around the world. In its announcement of the award, the Royal Swedish Academy of Sciences said, "Elinor Ostrom has challenged the conventional wisdom that common property is poorly managed and should be either regulated by central authorities or privatized."

Challenging conventional wisdom was not extraordinary for Lin Ostrom and her husband, Vincent,

A Commitment to Distinction

the Arthur F. Bentley Professor Emeritus of Political Science at Indiana University. Ordinary people, the Indiana University scholars had documented, were fully capable of sustaining and managing common resources through the creation of rules and institutions.

The Ostrom research agenda was a travel-intensive one and put Lin on the streets of Chicago, in the forests of Kenya, or on the oceans of the Pacific, according to John Graham, dean of the Indiana University School of Public and Environmental Affairs. Lin did "field studies of the world's fisheries, roamed with shepherds in Swiss pastures, and trudged around the Los Angeles water basin to distill the essentials of harnessing cooperation to overcome selfish interests," *Time* said of her work.

Here was someone who was open to any way you might get to a good answer. That's very rare. There was never anything conventional about her, and she didn't care about convention. She cared about answering questions, and she asked brilliant questions. She didn't care about what you had to study to answer them. She didn't care about how humble the subjects were. She just was able to take that genius for asking the right questions and follow the question wherever it went.

Lauren Robel
*Provost and Executive Vice President,
Indiana University*

Lin Ostrom was a woman of firsts. The first in her family to attend college. The first of four women admitted to UCLA's prestigious PhD economics program. One of the few women elected to two of the nation's most distinguished honorary academies: the National Academy of Sciences and the American Academy of Arts and Sciences.

And the first woman to ever receive the Nobel in economic sciences—a distinction that came as absolutely no surprise to those who monitored her career. But to Lin, the Nobel was another step in a lifelong journey marked by determination and commitment.

"Pursuing the kind of work I have been doing was not very much appreciated across the social sciences. But I just got fascinated with what I was doing and, being a stubborn son-of-a-gun, I just kept going. I had to learn very early about how to work hard and how to be independent," she said.

"When I was thinking of going to graduate school, I was strongly discouraged because I [as a woman] would never be able to do anything but teach in a city college," she explained in an interview with Adam Smith, editor-in-chief of Nobelprize.org, after the Nobel was announced. At the time, Lin explained, universities were simply not looking to invest in students who would end up teaching at city colleges.

"I've attended economic sessions where I've been the only woman in the room, but that is slowly changing," Lin told the Nobel editor. And then she added,

Facing
From One Generation to the Next. Elinor and Vincent Ostrom gave an important learning resource to Indiana University when they passed on their lifetime art collection. Today, the collection lives as a learning lab for students like Caroline Ferguson, a junior anthropology major at Indiana University, who interns at the Mathers Museum of World Cultures. The birch bark box in this photo was made by Rose Williams, an Ojibwe artist born in 1926. *Photo: Mathers Museum of World Cultures, Indiana University*

on the day she won the Nobel Prize and in her characteristically understated manner, "I would hope that the recognition here is helping that along."

Lin came to Indiana University in 1965 from California when Vincent was offered a full professorship. "I tagged along as it was very hard for any department to hire a woman in those days," she said.

That year, the IU political science department hired her to teach Introduction to American Government on Tuesday, Thursday, and Saturday mornings. The class met at 7:30 a.m., Lin noted of the less-than-coveted appointment. But she was named a visiting assistant professor to do that and taught IU freshmen for a year. After that, she was asked to be a graduate advisor, and the "visiting" portion of the title was removed.

The year 1965 was an interesting time to arrive on a Big Ten university campus. "We had eighty-five new graduate students a year and more than six hundred applications each year," Lin recalled in an interview published in the fall 2002 *Indiana University Research & Creative Activity*.

Some of those political science students were in school, in part, to avoid the draft, and some were inclined toward activism. "I had to get kids out of jail and write all sorts of letters for students who were doing well academically but who might not have been the most politic about what they were saying and how they were saying it," Lin said.

"It was an important period in the university's history, and I was glad to be a part of it, but there was no chance to do research." She was in the advisor position for three years and then accepted a regular faculty appointment in political science at IU.

In 1973, Lin and Vincent created what was their magnum opus both at Indiana University and in academe. The Workshop in Political Theory and Policy Analysis was designed as an interdisciplinary endeavor to bring scholars from economics, political science, and other social sciences together to understand how institutional arrangements affected performance of urban police agencies, irrigation systems, and forest resources.

Vincent named the new enterprise and chose the term "workshop" because it communicated his perspective of science as a form of collaborative artisanship. The interdisciplinary focus was to be the greatest distinction of the workshop, and one that both Vincent and Lin deemed critical to their research.

"If you're going to address some of the questions about how people govern very important resources, like our forests, can just a social scientist or just a forester address the question of how to stop deforestation? I say no," Lin explained.

Over time, the Ostroms studied more than two hundred forests around the world. Leading interdisciplinary teams, they learned the problems of people whose lives were dependent upon forests and explored how people monitored both each other and a forest's use.

Not only did Lin and Vincent create the workshop that was to become one of Indiana University's most widely known and respected institutes, but they also made substantial philanthropic gifts to IU to assure proper funding of the new initiative.

Kent E. Dove, who was vice president for development at the Indiana University Foundation, explained the Ostroms' rationale: "This was a relatively small component of the university, with support that was adequate, but not ample. Lin and Vincent knew that if they were going to achieve the full potential of the workshop and do what they dreamed of doing, putting their own money into the program made enormous sense."

"Lin was a bright, bright woman," Kent added, "not only as an academic, but in a very practical way."

Eileen Savage, formerly associate vice president of the Indiana University Foundation and now chief advancement officer at the Cranbrook Educational Community, said that the Ostroms' giving resulted in several distinct funds to support the workshop.

The primary fund, the Tocqueville Fund for the Study of Human Institutions, was named to honor Alexis de Tocqueville, whose portrayal of American society inspired the workshop's approach to institutional research. This fund, Eileen noted, encouraged independent research and helped establish a vital network of affiliated scholars around the world. In 2017, the workshop had nearly ninety external affiliate

Those who ultimately strengthen and truly advance a university do so through generosity of time, generosity of talent, and generosity of giving. Lin Ostrom was one such university builder who added loyalty to the list of what she gave to Indiana University.

David Zaret, dean of the Indiana University College of Arts and Sciences during much of Lin's tenure at IU, said of her: "When looking at her personnel file, one is astounded to see over forty-five years a nearly continuous record of invitations and solicitations by other institutions to come join faculties at Harvard, Michigan, and other prestigious institutions. But Lin consistently turned down all those institutions to remain a member of the faculty at the College of Arts and Sciences and to continue her work with her faculty colleagues and students."

I've been privileged in my career to meet some truly great people. In fact, the first person I ever interviewed was also a Nobel Laureate! But greatness rarely comes with such easygoing humanity and generosity of spirit as with Elinor Ostrom. I guess she wasn't born a Hoosier, but evidently she knew home when she'd found it.

Jane Pauley
Indiana University
Class of 1972

Again and again when one reads about the life of Lin Ostrom, two characteristics are consistent. First, she was unconventional. In style. In research. In the practical ways she lived. And in her academic life, where she was ultimately inclusive and engaging.

And second, she was remarkably adept at simplifying and getting things done efficiently and, characteristically, in a transparent manner.

So it was no surprise to Eileen Savage, Lin's development officer at the Indiana University Foundation, when Lin called her a few days after the Nobel Prize announcement. The phone call came early in the morning, Eileen recalls, and Lin was very straightforward: "I don't want to receive the Nobel Prize award money directly," she told Eileen. "If it comes to Indiana University, we can maximize the gift," as

individual taxes would not be taken from the award.

"This is what I want to accomplish," Lin told Eileen that fall day in 2009. "Will you work with the Nobel Prize Committee to make this happen?" she asked Eileen.

"Yes," came the answer from the development officer who had worked with the Ostroms to assure that their earlier gifts to IU had also been maximized for their beloved workshop.

In May 2012, IU renamed the workshop to honor the Ostroms. It became the Vincent and Elinor Ostrom Workshop in Political Theory and Policy Analysis. Today, with a nod to the casual, informal style that was Lin Ostrom, it's called, simply, the Ostrom Workshop most of the time.

"Lin would have been pleased," Eileen said.

faculty from countries as varying as India, Columbia, Poland, Sweden, Brazil, and Romania. Additionally, fifty-five Indiana University faculty members were affiliate workshop faculty in 2017.

Other funds, including the Ostrom Endowment Fund, the Workshop Research Chair for Visiting Scholars, the Skytte Fellowship Endowment, and the Workshop Graduate Fellowship, all support research

and visiting scholars and provide fellowships and scholarships in institutional analysis.

THE BROADER MESSAGE

"Do you have a message for the general public?" the Nobelprize.org interviewer asked Lin Ostrom in 2009.

She responded, "We need to get people away from the notion that you have to have a fancy car and a huge house. Why do humans need huge homes? I was born poor, and I didn't know you bought clothes at anything but Goodwill until I went to college," she said.

"Some of our mentality about what it means to have a good life is . . . I think . . . not going to help us in the next fifty years. We have to think through how to choose a meaningful life where we're helping one another in ways that really help the earth," she concluded.

Helping the earth, to Lin and Vincent, meant many things, but included, for sure, living simply. Their home on Lampkins Ridge Road in Bloomington, where they regularly hosted scholars and researchers from around the world, was furnished with furniture made by the Ostroms themselves, including a dining room table custom-crafted to be as large as the room could accommodate, according to Eileen Savage.

"They rarely ate alone," Eileen said. "There were always fellows, researchers, postdocs, students, alumni, and collaborators from around the world at the Ostrom table."

Lauren Robel, provost and executive vice president of Indiana University at the time of Lin's death in 2012, called her "an exemplary citizen of the Bloomington campus."

"She was extraordinarily generous with her intellectual gifts," Lauren said.

There are, particularly in the life of a prolific researcher, many ways to measure success. The author of thirty-two books, Lin served on more than twenty editorial boards and wrote more than three hundred journal articles and book chapters during her career. She served as national president of the American Political Science Association and held academic appointments in both the IU College of Arts and Sciences and the School of Public and Environmental Affairs.

I think Lin was one of those individuals who got more joy out of the success of her students than from her own personal success. It was a remarkable testament to her identity as a teacher.

Kent E. Dove
Vice President of Development,
Indiana University Foundation

Lin died at the age of seventy-eight of pancreatic cancer in June 2012 in Bloomington. Her beloved husband, Vincent, who was twelve years older than she, died seventeen days later.

The Indiana University community celebrated the lives of the Ostroms in October 2012 with a remembrance service at the Indiana University Auditorium. Two days later, "Reflections on the Ostroms" involved more than one hundred attendees from countries around the world who shared their professional and personal remembrances of Lin and Vincent.

One of the lasting tributes to this remarkable Indiana University faculty member came from the International Association for the Study of the Commons (IASC). The organization created the Elinor Ostrom

Nearly every summer beginning in 1967 and continuing through 2008, Lin and Vincent Ostrom drove to Manitoulin Island, Ontario, a Canadian island located in Lake Huron. In 1968, they constructed a simple, small log cabin on the island to use as a summer writing retreat.

At Manitoulin and, indeed, during all their excursions, the Ostroms built a distinguished collection of art and artifacts, with particular attention to traditional and contemporary work by North American Indians. Their collection featured a special focus on Ojibwe art, much of which was purchased on Manitoulin from indigenous artists and artisans.

The Ostroms collected boxes, baskets, pottery, prints, and paintings and brought the art and artifacts back to their Bloomington home.

They were intent on sharing the collection widely, and Vincent noted that "we may someday be able to make some useful additions to a university, provincial, or state museum in addition to the satisfaction that we . . . gain from collecting the baskets ourselves."

Sara Clark, a PhD student in folklore at Indiana University, is writing her dissertation, a biography of the Ostroms, with a focus on what she calls their "interdisciplinary living." Sara notes that the art and artifacts "were a means for the Ostroms to share their lives with people, an extension of their academic work, and another method of communal exchange."

"Their home was persistently in motion," Sara noted, as Lin and Vincent collected new holdings and frequently rearranged to accommodate the growing collection.

As part of their estate, the Ostroms left the collection of art and artifacts to Indiana University. Today, the Elinor and Vincent Ostrom Collection at the Mathers Museum of World Cultures on the IU Bloomington campus features objects from around the world and uncommon learning opportunities for today's students. In addition to the North American art, work from South America and Southeast Asia is represented in the collection.

Finding ways to always engage her students in hands-on work was supremely important to Lin Ostrom. Throughout her life, visitors to the Ostrom offices or home would meet students at the tables with Lin and Vincent. Discussing politics or economics, research projects or artistic expression—whatever the business of the day was—students were present.

Today, the art collection of the Ostroms continues to give what they gave in their lifetimes: hands-on learning experiences for undergraduate and graduate students at Indiana University.

Working in the Ostrom collection at the Mathers Museum offers opportunity to study the rich cultural expressions of North American Indians and to learn critical skills in curating and museum management.

Lin and Vincent Ostrom, clearly, planned carefully and well with their gift.

Award on the Collective Governance of Commons and biennially makes awards to young scholars, senior scholars, and practitioners.

In announcing the award, the IASC said of Lin, "Ostrom promoted a paradigm shift in political science and economics, as well as behavioral and social sciences in general."

Indiana University has lost an irreplaceable and magnificent treasure with the passing of Elinor Ostrom. Throughout her lifetime, Lin has brought distinction to the university through her groundbreaking work, which received the ultimate recognition in 2009 when she was awarded the Nobel Prize in Economic Sciences.

Michael A. McRobbie
President, Indiana University

A Commitment to International Experience

ADVANCING

GLOBAL PERSPECTIVE AT

INDIANA UNIVERSITY

"Deliver the world to IU students."

That was the vision of Herman B Wells, the legendary eleventh president of Indiana University.

Wells's deep appreciation for the global community led him to initiate IU's concerted efforts to become an international force in higher education. In the fall 2008 issue of *The Presidency*, a magazine of the American Council on Education, IU President Michael A. McRobbie wrote: "Over many years, Herman Wells succeeded in attracting world-class international faculty, . . . developing new international alliances with governments and institutions, establishing area studies programs, and dramatically expanding IU's foreign language curricula."

The twenty-first-century demands of higher education require, though, not just bringing the world to US students, but making and sustaining new commitments to engagement around the globe for both students and faculty. The Indiana University School of Global and International Studies was launched in 2015, combining IU's international studies departments, area and language studies programs, and research centers under one roof for the first time in the university's history.

"Whether the graduates of Indiana University," President McRobbie said, "are in Bloomington or Bangkok or Beijing, they will be living and working in a global environment that demands international educational experience."

Providing that international focus in a university education has long been both an honored tradition and a continuing commitment of Indiana University.

Photo: Indiana University Foundation

EDWARD L. HUTTON

A Catalyst for Global Experience

L et's make the world a better place."

It's such a simply stated intention. But for Edward L. Hutton, those few words summarized both the goal of his own life's work and what he coveted for Indiana University's brightest and best students.

What is it that sparks grand deeds of philanthropy? The experience of being needy? A deep determination to work hard and forge opportunity? Or is it a vision for change, a pursuit of better realities?

For Ed Hutton, a giant of a man born in 1919 to a family of nine children in the small, limestone town of Bedford, Indiana, it was all three.

DEFINED BY WORK AND GOOD FORTUNE

The Great Depression of the 1930s left Ed Hutton's father, a home builder, without work. Ed, even as young as eight or nine, became accustomed to rolling up his sleeves and chipping in to bring precious small income to his family. "I knocked and knocked on doors until I found work to do. I spaded gardens, mowed lawns at ten cents an hour, carried newspapers, sold magazines and donuts door-to-door," he said.

When he graduated from high school in 1936, Ed received several awards for leadership and one award he did not see coming: a $130 county scholarship to Indiana University. Ed's story, in many ways, became intertwined with IU from that point.

The young Hutton accepted the scholarship and enrolled at IU in the fall of 1936. To help pay his way through school, he became a student worker for the inimitable Herman B Wells, then dean of the IU School of Business and soon to become the eleventh president of Indiana University.

I don't know if [choosing to accept the IU scholarship] was the most important decision of my life, but I think it probably was. Other friends who did not attend college, but who opted to take whatever jobs they could find, ended up with non-spectacular careers.

Ed Hutton

In his senior year at IU, Ed received a bit of counsel from Arthur M. Weimer, then dean of the IU School of Business: Take the civil service examination.

"Four hours on a Saturday afternoon?" Ed asked himself. But Dean Weimer talked about the need to be "qualified and prepared" for many different scenarios that might arise in Ed's life, given that the United States was on the verge of its second world war.

Ed signed up for the exam and later said that doing so "probably saved my life." He scored well on the test and was informed by the Civil Service Commission that he was qualified to be a junior professional economist if he ever sought government employment.

When Ed graduated from IU with a bachelor's degree in business in 1940, he and his best friend, Walt Robbins, determined that the coming war limited their prospects for good employment. So they both enrolled in IU's graduate business program; Ed received his master's degree in 1941, and Walt received his in 1943. Afterward, both went to work for local businesses, biding time until the inevitable draft notices arrived.

In the most improbable coincidence, Ed received—on exactly the same day—the postcard draft notice and a telegram from the president of the United States. The postcard instructed him to report to his local draft office. The telegram explained that Ed had been selected to serve as a junior economist with the new Office of Emergency Management in Washington, DC, to help gear up for the coming war.

Holding two official communiqués from the federal government, Ed was perplexed. He located the address of the Bloomington draft board manager and walked over to his house. Again, with extraordinary luck, he found the man sitting on his front porch. Ed introduced himself and said, "Sir, I received these two communications today. Which would you recommend I follow?"

The head of the draft board, as Ed recalls, said, "Hell, son, if they need you that badly down in Washington, you send them a telegram today and tell them you're coming. And as for the draft notice there, give it to me, I'll take care of that."

"That's a defining moment. I call that luck. An amazing coincidence," Ed later said of that day in his young life.

So Ed went to Washington and joined the US Army in May 1943. His friend Walt had already joined at the end of 1942, and the two went through the ranks as privates, PFCs, corporals, and, finally, officer candidates. As Army men, the two Indiana soldiers faced experience after experience that taught them invalu-

Facing

A Place Apart. Ed Hutton dreamed of a learning space that resembled the finest small colleges of Europe when the Hutton Honors College was in the design stage. IU students (*l–r*) Maria del Valle Coello, Haily Merritt, and Jack Zhang are in the library, one of the coziest spots in the Hutton Honors College on the corner of Seventh and Woodburn on the Indiana University Bloomington campus. *Photo: Tyagan Miller*

able lessons in leadership. After the war, Ed was invited to become the deputy director of the Joint Import-Export Agency, negotiating trade agreements with several countries to help rebuild the German economy. In Berlin, he met up with Herman Wells again, who was serving as cultural affairs advisor with the US Office of Military Government in West Germany to begin to rebuild German educational programs, specifically the Free University of Berlin.

Ed, who had persuaded Walt to join him in Berlin, served as the deputy director of the Joint Import-Export Agency from 1946 to 1948, and the two managers eventually built an enterprise of ten thousand employees and directed West Germany's foreign trade. "Those experiences profoundly changed my life. Those years of living and working abroad were key to my development as a person and my success as a businessman," Ed said about his years in Germany.

After his Army service, Ed moved to New York in 1948 and continued to work in international trade as vice president and director of the World Commerce Corporation. In 1951, he joined W. R. Grace & Co., where he became a senior officer and director. Returning to the Midwest in the 1970s, he became founder, president, chief executive officer, and eventually chairman of Chemed and Omnicare, two international businesses that he described as "grandchildren" of W. R. Grace & Co. Not surprisingly, Ed's

longtime IU friend, Herman Wells, served as a director of both corporations from their very beginning.

CALLED BY HIS ALMA MATER

In the 1980s, Indiana University was preparing to honor its esteemed chancellor and Ed Hutton's most significant mentor, Herman B Wells, with the establishment of the Wells Scholars Program. IU envisioned an ambitious initiative that would attract the nation's best and brightest students, offering full tuition and fees, a living stipend, research grants, and international travel opportunities for four years of undergraduate study at IU Bloomington. The bold goal was to raise $20 million to fund endowments that would annually permit between eighteen and twenty-two incoming freshmen to be selected as Wells Scholars.

One of the critical needs IU faced in launching the Wells Scholars campaign was to identify a dynamic, inspired volunteer to chair the fundraising drive. IU Foundation president Curt Simic and former president Bill Armstrong approached Ed Hutton with a request to lead the campaign. The two outlined the campaign's goals and discussed Ed's potential role as a volunteer chair. Ed's response was firm and quick: "Of course, I'll do it."

Ed thus became the volunteer leader of a fundraising drive to build a scholarship program that today stands among the most competitive and prestigious honors awards offered by any American university. Throughout the Wells Scholars campaign, Ed remained highly engaged and frequently traveled to Bloomington from his corporate headquarters in Cincinnati, Ohio. He began a long tradition of making gifts in the name of a friend or colleague to honor that individual and encourage others to support the campaign.

The result was a fundraising effort that exceeded its original goal and concluded with $23 million raised. On Chancellor Wells's ninetieth birthday, June 7, 1992, the Wells Scholars Program was presented to the beloved IU leader from his many friends and admirers, including one of his former student workers, Ed Hutton.

AN INVITATION TO WORLD CITIZENSHIP

Ed Hutton was clearly motivated to bring about change in the world around him. And he communicated his objective to those at the IU Foundation who were working on the Wells Scholars campaign with him, including Rod Kirsh, then senior vice president for development, and Curt Simic.

Curt recollects the day that he said to Ed, "Time and again, you have mentioned how your experience in Germany helped you evolve from a small-town Hoosier boy into a person aware of the entire world."

"How do we make other small-town Hoosiers citizens of the world?" Ed asked.

Curt responded, "What if you found a way for IU students to have international experiences?"

"But how could that be possible with a student body of more than thirty thousand?" Ed asked.

Curt's suggestion was to consider the Honors Division because it was comprised of the top 10 percent of the IU student body and cut across every academic discipline at the university. Ed latched on to the idea, and the two next met with Lou Miller, the director of the Indiana University Honors Division. Lou spoke of the quality of the students and of the limited resources available to encourage students to take advantage of IU's worldwide linkages.

From there, it was a matter of figuring how much endowment it would take to provide a stipend for travel and enrollment in programs already in place at IU. Curt recalls, "It was not practical to support all Honors Division students in the same year, so we recommended that at some time during their four undergraduate years, honors students would be given the opportunity to apply for a grant under the Edward L. Hutton International Experiences Program."

Given the opportunity and the tools to work with, young people can accomplish miracles. They can do wonders.

Ed Hutton

Public universities, including IU, can be the cradle of what Thomas Jefferson called "the natural aristocracy," the grounds of which were not wealth and privilege but virtue and talents. Mr. Hutton himself is proof of that Jeffersonian faith, achieving what he did through talent and hard work, and now he is giving opportunities for development and achievement to others.

Karen Hanson
Senior Vice President for Academic Affairs and Provost, University of Minnesota; Former Provost and Dean, Hutton Honors College

Ed realized his dream by helping students realize world citizenship. More than five hundred students typically incorporate international experience into their annual academic programs at Indiana University through the Hutton International Experiences Program. Since its inception, nearly 6,400 students have participated in the program. In recognition of the generosity that created the International Experiences Program, Indiana University renamed its Honors Division the Hutton Honors College.

Ed loved visiting Bloomington and would go to the Honors College offices on the corner of Seventh and Jordan streets—two small houses with administrative offices and student lounges for IU's most highly qualified students. And students loved visiting with Mr. Hutton. In him, students found what might have been surprising for a captain of industry. He was not a hard-driven, bang-on-the-table kind of leader.

Ed Hutton has added new meaning to President Herman Wells's statement that the campus of Indiana University is not just in Bloomington, not just in Indiana, or in the United States, but extends around the globe. He has helped our students become citizens of the world, and for that he has our enduring gratitude.

Adam W. Herbert
President, Indiana University

"Ed was so strongly influenced by Herman Wells, and, consistently, he saw Wells build consensus rather than make demands," Curt said.

When they met Ed Hutton, IU students encountered a gentle person who was intently interested in their development. His interest, always, was to create opportunity. Ed would sit in the afternoons and students would come and tell him about their international experiences. He just loved it, Curt recalls, and no doubt it was inspirational on both sides.

THE CAPSTONE GIFT

During one of Ed's visits to campus, Curt picked him up at the Hutton Honors College and was driving him to another meeting. Ed had spent the afternoon in one of the small honors houses, the crowded, refashioned locale that did not, from any perspective, seem like an appropriate home for the "best and brightest."

Halfway across campus, Ed turned to Curt and said, "You know, Curt, if it's going to have my name on it, I'd like a nicer building." And he added, "And I'm happy to pay for it."

Ed became intimately involved in the design of the building and dreamed of a facility that resembled the finest smaller colleges of Europe, with open space and many windows to assure good light. A young architect from Indianapolis, Daryl Williams-Dotson of WDI Architecture, was engaged by IU vice president and chief administrative officer Terry Clapacs to design the building. The first woman and the first African American architect selected to design a Bloomington campus building, Daryl proposed a sophisticated, two-story collegiate gothic structure that both complemented the nearby residential neighborhood and harmonized with the limestone architecture of the old campus.

Ed frequently came to campus to meet with Daryl and the team leading the design and construction of the newest—and what was to become one of the most attractive—buildings on the Bloomington campus.

Ed Hutton had an incredible can-do approach to life and learning. If we can channel just a fraction of his energy, wisdom, and commitment to academic excellence and public service in the lessons we teach at the Hutton Honors College, we will be successful.

Matt Auer
Dean, School of Public and International Affairs, University of Georgia; Former Dean, Hutton Honors College

Ed's dreams and aspirations for the next generation blended beautifully with IU's ambitions to house the Hutton Honors College in an attractive, accessible, and comfortable space. Curt's role, as an IU fundraising officer, was a simple one: "To listen to those aspirations and help Ed find the program at IU that made it possible for him to realize his vision."

Those who worked closely with Curt and other IU leaders learned—time and again—that the most important attribute a university representative can have is the ability to listen, to resist the temptation to sell what an organization may want at the expense of not hearing a donor's own passion. "I have a ceramic ear—a big one—in my office that I refer to whenever I meet new development officers," Curt explained. "My advice is always simple: Listen for what means the most to donors and then design something that speaks to their dreams and connects to the university's strategic plan."

Ed Hutton died in Cincinnati on March 3, 2009. The weekend before his death, he visited the Hutton Honors College to see the fresh landscaping just completed in anticipation of the building's dedication on April 8. Ed did not live to see the dedication and formal opening, but in the late winter of that year, he did have the opportunity to tour the finished building.

A DEFINING MOMENT

In a conversation one day about what was to become the Edward L. Hutton International Experiences

I will forever cherish his lessons, his stories of hard work and success, his enthusiasm for my career, and his great love for Indiana University and her students.

IU Student
Maria Gramelspacher
Studied in Honduras
Spring 2004

Program, Curt asked Ed an all-important question: "What if you found a way for IU students to have international experiences like you did?"

Ed Hutton lived a "what if?" life. Through his vision of change and his commitment to foster international understanding, honors students at Indiana University today—and for generations to come—will become citizens of the world, with all the experience, exposure, and opportunity Ed coveted for them.

Mr. Hutton's life is an example of the amazing things that can be accomplished with determination and hard work. What makes him a truly great man is that he shared his successes. He gave back to his community and allowed so many students, like myself, to travel overseas and gain valuable life experiences.

IU Student Rebecca R. Baxter
Studied in Japan Summer 2005

A Commitment to Medical Research

IMPROVING

WOMEN'S HEALTH AT

INDIANA UNIVERSITY

Cancer research or athletics? Libraries or new trees? Professorships or theatrical troupes?

The process of choosing where to make gifts in a complex public academic institution like Indiana University naturally begins with a donor's own experience. And the essential act of linking that experience to an organization's goals is at the very core of every relationship between benefactors and institutions that becomes productive and long-lived.

John W. Gardner, the founder of Common Cause, noted that philanthropists, when they choose where to give gifts, are commonly addressing society's most urgent priorities: "Wealth is not new. Neither is charity. But the idea of using private wealth imaginatively, constructively, and systematically to attack the fundamental problems of mankind is new."

For philanthropists who choose to have an impact in a realm related to—and in many cases made possible through—higher education, the list of potential giving opportunities on a campus seems never-ending. At Indiana University, it begins, of course, with students, but quickly expands to those teaching, to those whose lives and circumstances are studied in classrooms and laboratories, and to those who research society's most critical issues, encompassing both the breadth and magnitude of the university's mission, vision, and outreach.

Photo: Indiana University Foundation

PATRICIA R. MILLER

"Yet to Come"

The question was a simple one: "What gift to IU has brought you the greatest happiness?" Patricia R. Miller, a 1960 graduate of Indiana University, paused for a moment and then said, simply: "It's yet to come."

No answer could better capture the personality and perspective of this Indiana University alumna who has had a singular impact at her alma mater through both her corporate and personal philanthropy.

For Pat Miller, the best is yet to come. And she makes it clear that the phrase is more than a slogan: It's a way of looking at life as potential, as opportunity, and as promise. It's also a way of thinking with a future focus, an orientation that invites anticipation of all that is still to come in life . . . regardless of all that has been accomplished.

AN EARLY LOVE FOR BUSINESS

The story of Pat Miller is both inspired and inspiring. It begins with her upbringing in Farmington, a small farm town of two thousand west of Peoria in central Illinois. The community was home to both of Pat's grandparents. Her Grandfather Polito, a Sicilian immigrant, ran a small grocery story in Farmington, and her Grandfather Willard was a farmer in the community.

In high school, Pat worked at her grandfather's grocery store, attaining her first introduction to the business world. "We had everything a big corporation has: Customer service, inventory control, and bookkeeping. And early in the mornings, I would ride with my grandfather up to Chicago to get the produce and bring it back to Farmington," Pat explains.

"I loved that work, and I loved being in business," she says of those days. "I learned early in life that I loved working. And I have loved working my entire life."

"I grew up in what I thought was an ideal place: I had the grocery store to work in, I had the farm, and then, in high school, I worked at the town movie theater, so I got to see all the movies and have all the popcorn I could eat!" Pat said.

Near the end of her high school days, Pat and her mother drove to the neighboring state to visit the Indiana University campus in Bloomington. Both Pat's aunt and uncle had attended IU, and her mother was thinking that it might be a good option for Pat, too.

"That one day was a deal sealer," Pat recalls. "I just loved the campus. It was so perfect—back in the day, it took us nearly eight hours to drive there. I wanted to go away to school, and I was completely sold on IU after that visit."

Pat loved sports, and, even though schools had no formal athletic programs for girls at the time, she played softball and half-court basketball at noon and after school. She enrolled at IU as a physical education major, but the lab classes were quite time-intensive, she said. Talking with her uncle during a holiday break, she began to consider switching her major to business.

"I changed to business education, because I wasn't thinking far enough outside the box to think I could

actually be in business. I thought I could only teach business," she explains.

After graduating from IU, Pat taught high school in Indiana, first in Hammond, then back in Bloomington so her husband, Mike, could finish law school. Next they moved to Indianapolis, and finally Fort Wayne, where the couple settled.

In Fort Wayne, Pat was on the neighborhood welcoming committee and once went to visit a new resident. Barbara Bradley Baekgaard had recently moved to Fort Wayne from Chicago and was hanging wallpaper in her new home that day. Barbara greeted Pat at the door and asked, "Do you know how to hang wallpaper?"

"No," Pat replied.

"Come on in, I'll teach you," Barbara said.

Pat and Barbara's first business, Up Your Wall, was the result of that visit. The two became fast friends and began wallpapering, first in friends' homes and then around Fort Wayne. "We were a great team—Barbara liked papering around the doors and windows and I liked doing the straight walls," Pat said.

In 1982, the wallpapering business partners were traveling home to Indiana from a trip to Florida and had a layover in the Atlanta airport. "We noticed," Barbara said, "no one was carrying anything colorful or fun."

The result of their observation? Vera Bradley, Inc., a manufacturer of cotton, quilted, floral bags. And,

eventually, an initial public offering of stock, more than three thousand employees, and a presence in gift shops and stores around the world.

A GRAND IDEA

The Vera Bradley success story is a classic tale of a good idea meeting American entrepreneurial spirit. The two friends began the business in Barbara's basement and bought their first cloth at the local fabric store. They cut out patterns for a bag on a ping-pong table and ran an ad in the local paper to hire people who could sew at home. Then they delivered sewing kits with patterns, fabric, and thread, along with a prototype of the bag, to the home workers.

One woman who sewed at home began working on her enclosed porch with the kits and eventually developed her own company to sew for Vera Bradley. And the women shared their idea and early products with friends and family around the country.

One such friend, Mary Sloan, was Barbara's college roommate and lived outside Washington, DC. Pat and Barbara sent her a bag and asked, "Do you like this?"

"Oh, I love it!" came the response.

"Good. We'll give you 15 percent of everything you sell. Go out and sell it!" was the agreement. And so Mary began selling Vera Bradley bags in the DC area.

That's how the sales force was built: a friend would stop in to say hi, and, Pat says, "We wouldn't let her go."

"Enthusiasm breeds enthusiasm," Pat said, and early on, it was clear that the two Fort Wayne women had come up with a grand idea. Women liked the bags and began buying them. In very large numbers.

PAYING TRIBUTE TO A FRIEND

In 1993, Mary Sloan lost her battle with breast cancer. Pat said, "There was no question that we wanted to do something in Mary's memory to address women's health and, specifically, to address breast cancer research."

And Vera Bradley was beginning to have earnings that permitted the company to begin to give philanthropically. "So we started," Pat said.

The Vera Bradley Classic, a golf and tennis tournament for women, was launched that year as a fundraiser to honor the memory of Mary Sloan, one of the first sales reps for Vera Bradley. "When we first started the golf tournament, we wanted to have one of the country's best tournaments for women," Pat said.

That phrase is a precise definition of the Vera Bradley Classic today. In 2018, the Classic will celebrate its twenty-fifth anniversary as the women's largest amateur golf and tennis charity event in the United States. At the 2017 Classic, over four hundred athletes, five hundred volunteers, and eight hundred dinner guests attended. Since its founding the Classic has raised more than $30 million for breast cancer research.

The Classic led Pat and Barbara to found the Vera Bradley Foundation. And it also led to a twenty-five-

AND THE NAME?

So who is this woman named Vera Bradley?

"When we began making bags, we were looking for a name that had a certain style and was easy to say and remember," Pat Miller said.

Vera Bradley was Barbara Bradley Baekgaard's mother's name. "It was the perfect fit," Pat said.

"My mother's name is Wilma Polito," Pat added. "It just didn't have that ring."

year relationship with the Indiana University School of Medicine. Barbara and Pat had looked at various organizations that were best situated to aggressively pursue new research initiatives when they decided to honor Mary by funding breast cancer research. They selected the Cancer Center at the Indiana University School of Medicine in Indianapolis.

Today the Vera Bradley Foundation for Breast Cancer Research Laboratories at the School of Medicine are recognized by the National Cancer Institute for meeting all rigorous criteria for state-of-the art multidisciplinary cancer research. The laboratories in Indianapolis offer the only site in Indiana that introduces first-to-human drugs into treatment.

The long-term commitment to be a philanthropic partner in the fight against breast cancer has produced highly regarded dialogue and engagement between the leaders of the Vera Bradley Foundation and the physicians and researchers of the IU School of Medicine. Visits to Indianapolis from Fort Wayne are frequent, and the staff of the foundation takes every opportunity to learn and understand the significance of the work underway at the Vera Bradley Foundation for Breast Cancer Research Laboratories.

Pat is a brilliant businesswoman and one of the warmest, most gracious people I know. She and her colleagues from the Vera Bradley Foundation come down regularly to visit the research laboratories. They know the investigators by name—and they actually greet them with hugs! They're—in every way—partners in this whole mission to improve care for breast cancer patients.

Jay L. Hess
*MD, MHSA, Dean, Indiana University
School of Medicine*

Currently, the Vera Bradley Foundation funds four distinct avenues to improve care for patients of breast cancer at the IU Simon Cancer Center:

· More than thirty physicians and scientists work to produce better outcomes for patients of breast cancer through prevention, treatment, and cures.

Patricia R. Miller

· Monogrammed Medicine focuses on tailoring therapy for breast cancer patients so the right therapies are given to the right patients at the right time.
· Four academic chairs attract top faculty and investigators to lead the program:

– Vera Bradley Chair in Oncology
– Vera Bradley Foundation Chair in Breast Cancer Innovation
– Vera Bradley Foundation Chair in Breast Cancer Research
– Vera Bradley Foundation Chair in Breast Cancer Discovery

· The Vera Bradley Foundation Scholars program trains postdoctoral researchers from around the globe to advance knowledge of breast cancer and improve care for women.

"We want to continue to find new ways of attacking this horrible disease," Pat says, and that commitment requires a posture of learning and listening.

"We go to the experts at the IU Simon Cancer Center and ask what they are working on and what we should be funding next," Pat explains. "The disease is so complex but the people here are committed to helping women live breast cancer free. We stand together with them in that goal," she adds.

THE GIFT OF SERVICE

Sharing her expertise has been, throughout her career, another path to giving for Pat Miller.

Her love for sports—both as a participant and a spectator—led to her service on the Indiana University Varsity Club National Board of Directors. She was a member of the IU Foundation Board of Directors for fourteen years, a member of the Jacobs School of Music Dean's Advisory Board, and also a founding member of the IU Women's Philanthropy Leadership Council.

What distinguished the way Pat Miller did business, both in the private and public sectors, and served her alma mater as a volunteer leader? The simplest adages take on new meaning when you talk with Pat. Phrases like "treat people like you want to be treated" have meaning to her across all the sectors in which she has worked.

"This was so important to our business success, because most of our co-workers were women, and they had much bigger jobs at home than they did during the daytime. We understood, from the very beginning, that these women went home to families after work and had dinner to get on the table and homework to do with their kids," Pat said.

"While we have made major strides in the treatment of breast cancer, the reality is that today's therapies are still inadequate," Indiana University School of Medicine Dean Jay L. Hess said in June 2018 at the twenty-fifth annual Vera Bradley Foundation for Breast Cancer Classic in Fort Wayne, Indiana. "Far too many women still die from this disease, and others endure long-lasting side effects from treatments. We owe it to women everywhere to do better," Dean Hess added.

At the Classic, the IU School of Medicine announced the launch of the Vera Bradley Foundation Center for Breast Cancer Research, dedicated to improving therapies for breast cancers that are especially difficult to treat.

With a focus on triple-negative breast cancer, the research center is funded by a new gift from the Vera Bradley Foundation that was matched both by IU and the IU School of Medicine.

"Cure is a bold word," Dean Hess said. "But we really believe this is possible. We don't expect to eradicate all forms of triple-negative breast cancer in the immediate future, but we do think we can identify subsets that are particularly vulnerable to these new types of therapies. And what we learn will help us continue to improve treatments for other women."

There are, indeed, other golden rules in Pat Miller's life. "Be passionate about what you do, and surround yourself with passionate people," Pat says. "There is absolutely no substitute for enthusiasm."

Continuous improvement is one that Pat describes as a "given, forever."

"You don't stop improving. Ever and always, better yourself and your company," she says.

Did the young woman from Farmington ever imagine the business success she achieved in life? Did she think her handbags and accessories would be seen on *Desperate Housewives* and *Brothers and Sisters* and in more than twenty feature-length films?

"No," Pat says. "Never."

And she adds, in her characteristically understated manner, "but somehow we're here. And I couldn't be happier."

INSPIRED GIVING

Pat Miller officially retired from Vera Bradley in 2012, and she and her husband, Mike, now divide their time between Indiana and Arizona. She remains a member of the boards of directors of both Vera Bradley, Inc. and the Vera Bradley Foundation.

Her legacy as a businesswoman touches private, public, and nonprofit sectors. And yet her giving is not finished, as she's quick to tell you.

Patricia R. Miller

FROM PRIVATE TO PUBLIC SECTORS

Pat Miller's expertise as a business-woman merged into the public sector when the governor of the state of Indiana, Mitch Daniels, asked her to take a two-year leave of absence from her private endeavors in 2005.

Daniels, now president of Purdue University, asked Pat to serve in his cabinet as Indiana's first-ever secretary of commerce and CEO of the Indiana Economic Development Corporation. She accepted the invitation and took a leave of absence from Vera Bradley to help attract and support new business with the goal of creating new jobs in Indiana.

"That was an amazing experience," Pat said of her time as a state employee. "I traveled the state extensively and visited so many different companies—everything from a two-person, mom-and-pop shop to Rolls Royce, with more than a million square feet and some four thousand employees in Indianapolis."

"It was an unbelievable experience of Americana. I've never worked as hard in my life, and I absolutely loved it," she concluded.

Some time ago, as a member of the Women's Philanthropy Leadership Council at Indiana University, Pat heard University Landscape Architect Mia Williams speak about landscaping on the Bloomington campus. Specifically, Mia addressed recent efforts with campus gateways and the extension of Woodlawn Avenue.

Mia connected many of the newer landscape initiatives at IU to the dreams of Herman B Wells. In 1962, Dr. Wells, in an address to IU alumni, said, "I hope our alumni will always insist upon retention of our precious islands of green and serenity—our most important physical asset, transcending even classrooms, libraries, and laboratories in their ability to inspire students to dream long dreams of future usefulness and achievement—dreams that are an important and essential part of the undergraduate experience."

Mia Williams was speaking "directly to me" that day, Pat said. "When Mia talks about garden and green space design, you are inspired, and it's so easy to catch her enthusiasm," Pat added.

So Pat, the IU alumna who fell in love with the beauty of IU Bloomington on that first visit over six decades ago, listened and learned about campus beautification.

THOMAS M. LOFTON

Philanthropy's Faithful Steward

There are certain moments in the history of educational institutions that define character, commitment, and capability over the longer term. The grants received from Lilly Endowment Inc. for pervasive computing, combined with major funding from the National Science Foundation, enabled Indiana University to move ahead in one of its most innovative and monumental technology initiatives and position itself as a global leader in information technology.

Lilly Endowment's funding from 1999 through 2014 advanced pervasive technology at Indiana University in several primary channels. Under the leadership of then vice president for information technology and chief information officer Michael A. McRobbie, the initiatives sparked new creativity and innovation in science and scholarship. Multiple new software platforms were developed that addressed topics as varied as Shakespearean vocabularies, cybercrime, and smartphone applications.

Students, at both the graduate and undergraduate levels, found exceptionally rich research experiences in technology and translational scholarship through the initiatives. A distinctly high-tech environment at both Indiana University Bloomington and Indiana University Purdue University Indianapolis (IUPUI) helped create new jobs and businesses in Indiana.

And last, the investment in pervasive technology dramatically cultivated outreach and grant activity at Indiana University. Over the time of the Lilly grants, Pervasive Technology Institute researchers collectively published 1,059 works in peer-reviewed journals, conferences, and books. Scientists registered thirty-five inventions with IU and distributed 178 releases of open-source software programs. *Security Matters* was developed as a quick, easy-to-understand video series to inform the public about practical steps to enhance cyber security, generating a total of 1,230 segments focused on topics as diverse as mobile banking, strong passwords, and privacy protection. A total of 274 online services, including new data analysis tools and databases, were made available on the web for use in scientific and scholarly endeavors.

"TAKE WHAT YOU FIND HERE"

Colonel Eli Lilly, the eminent chemist and Civil War officer, founded the pharmaceutical giant Eli Lilly and Company in 1876. When his son, J. K. Lilly Sr., joined the company in 1882, Colonel Lilly gave him wise counsel: "Take what you find here and make it better and better."

In the midst of the Great Depression in 1937, J. K. Lilly Sr., and his sons, Eli and J. K. Jr., incorporated Lilly Endowment with funding from their Eli Lilly and Company stock.

Colonel Lilly's advice to his son was eventually carved on the walls of the Eli Lilly and Company international headquarters in Indianapolis. And, for one of the Hoosier state's most distinguished citizens, Tom Lofton, the time-tested admonition became the raison d'être of his career.

The longtime leader of Lilly Endowment Inc., Tom had a style of living, and of giving, that was the antithesis of extravagance. He lived, he worked, and he gave in a style that was private, analytical, and reflective.

Most frequently described by those who knew him best as "very circumspect," Tom had broad reach and impact as Lilly Endowment grew to one of the largest private foundations in the country, with $10.1 billion in assets at the end of 2014.

> *Tom Lofton's public-mindedness with respect to advancing the quality of life in the capital city has touched the lives of virtually every citizen of our community.*
>
> *Gerald Bepko*
> *Vice President for Long-Range Planning, Indiana University, and Chancellor, Indiana University Purdue University Indianapolis*

HOOSIER ROOTS

The path to leadership for Tom Lofton began in the neighborhood of Irvington on the east side of Indianapolis, where he was reared. Tom grew up in the Christian Church (Disciples of Christ), and after graduation from Howe High School, he enrolled at Butler University. There he met his life partner, Betty, and the two began a seven-year courtship that lasted throughout college and law school. Betty went on to graduate from Butler, but Tom transferred to Indiana University in Bloomington after his freshman year.

"We waited to marry until Tom finished law school," Betty said. That meant marriage in 1954, after Tom's graduation with distinction from the IU School of Law. The young Loftons moved to Washington,

DC, where Tom served as a law clerk for Supreme Court Justice Sherman Minton. Next was a three-year term in the Judge Advocate General's Corps in the US Army and then back home to Indiana.

Tom accepted a position at the Indianapolis law firm of Baker & Daniels (now Faegre Baker Daniels) in 1955, with a focus in corporate and antitrust law. In the late 1960s, in response to the growing influence of nonprofit organizations in the country, Tom added charitable and philanthropic organizations to his areas of focus.

In 1970, Tom was named chief legal counsel to Lilly Endowment as a Baker & Daniels senior partner. He developed a personal acquaintance with two of the Endowment's founders, J. K. Lilly Jr. and Eli Lilly, and began to learn firsthand about the founders' values and intentions through philanthropy in community development, education, and religion.

Betty and Tom lived on the north side of Indianapolis for the thirty-six years he was at Baker & Daniels, and Tom drove downtown to his office each morning. Betty remembers one day that was different from Tom's predictable routine: "He came back home midmorning that day, after a meeting with Tom Lake, the Lilly Endowment chairman. I was surprised to see him, but then he said to me, 'Tom Lake wants me to come to the Endowment. Permanently. And I think I will do that.'"

Tom retired from Baker & Daniels and joined Lilly Endowment as vice chairman in 1991. He was named chairman in 1993.

When he accepted the leadership of Lilly Endowment, Tom stepped into a role that would consume the rest of his professional life. He became an extraordinary steward of the legacy of the Endowment's founders. That stewardship included a single-minded commitment to their ideals, their standards, and their intentions and led to great professional and personal satisfaction for Tom.

Betty tells a story about one of the more significant initiatives that Lilly Endowment supported while Tom was chairman, "Giving Funds for Tomorrow" (GIFT), which began in 1990. Eventually, GIFT supported the development and flourishing of community foundations in every one of Indiana's ninety-two counties and the emergence of those foundations as civic forces to improve quality of life in Indiana.

"Tom was so proud of those foundations. He talked about what they were accomplishing, both large and small investments that were very significant to communities around the state," Betty said. One day, Tom came home from work and on their regular evening walk around their neighborhood, he told Betty that one of the foundations had provided money for a fire truck, something the community sorely needed for public safety. "Isn't that wonderful? They needed a fire truck and that community got exactly what it needed to improve safety there," he said.

During his twenty-two-year career as leader of Lilly Endowment, the organization distributed more than $7 billion in grants. The impact Tom had on the Endowment's work during those years, according to Clay Robbins, current board chairman and Tom's successor, was "incalculable."

"Tom had a style of work and thinking based in analysis and process. He had a large presence in my life as a mentor and taught me that because the world is an imperfect one, I must always think deeper and use my best judgment," Clay said.

> *Like the Eagle Scout he was in his youth,*
> *Tom excelled at being prepared.*
> *Thoroughly. And always.*
>
> *Clay Robbins*
> *Chairman, President & Chief Executive*
> *Officer, Lilly Endowment Inc.*

Throughout his college and law school days, Tom developed a deep affection and loyalty to both Indiana University and its beloved chancellor, Herman B Wells, a Sigma Nu fraternity brother. Curt Simic, president emeritus of the Indiana University Foundation, recalls a lesson of thoughtfulness he learned from Tom about how to honor people like Dr. Wells, who was responsible for building the alma mater both Tom and Curt loved.

"When he drove to Bloomington, Tom often stopped at Gray Brothers Cafeteria in Mooresville to buy a freshly baked pie for Dr. Wells—a man whose love for pies was no secret. Later, when Dr. Wells was unable to attend meetings of the Endowment's board of directors because of his health, Tom frequently drove to Bloomington with both a pie and a meeting agenda in hand," Curt said.

"There are so many, many ways—that far exceed dollars—that donors contribute to and strengthen institutions," Curt said. "Tom taught through his own style of leadership and by actively modeling impact and influence. His gifts of leadership to Indiana University were beyond measure."

Tom's loyalty to IU eventually led to his founding of the School of Law's Board of Visitors. He was president of the Law Alumni Association in 1976 and received a Distinguished Alumni Service Award from IU in 1997. The honorary Doctor of Laws was awarded to Tom in 2000 by IU President Myles Brand.

THE IMPACT OF LEADERSHIP

William G. Enright, a longtime member of Lilly Endowment's Board of Directors, is director emeritus of the Lake Institute on Faith and Giving at the Lilly Family School of Philanthropy at IUPUI. Bill knew Tom well and believed that Tom's tenure as chairman of Lilly Endowment was aptly characterized by three distinctive interests:

· Broad investments in religion, where Tom's personal journey and life of faith were reflected;
· Loyalty to higher education generally, and Indiana University specifically;
· Emphasis on the importance of local communities in Indiana to address quality-of-life issues for their citizens.

I can think of no living alumnus who has been more loyal or achieved greater distinction than Thomas M. Lofton.

Herman B Wells

The value of mentoring, in any profession, is immeasurable—and enduring. In a field like fundraising, it is most critical, Curt Simic believes.

"With good mentors, younger development officers learn how business is done, certainly. But more importantly, they witness relationships and transactions that have been built on integrity and honor," Curt said.

"Tom Lofton was one of the most significant mentors in my professional life," Curt said. Curt and Tom became trusted colleagues when Curt returned to Indiana University from the West Coast to lead the IU Foundation in 1988. At the time, Tom was a member of the IU Foundation Board of Directors and chaired its Legal Affairs Committee.

Curt recalls vividly when he first realized how significant the counsel to a CEO from a board member such as Tom Lofton could be.

IU, before Curt's arrival at the IU Foundation, had accepted the gift of a Mississippi cattle farm with the stipulation that cattle farming would continue on the property. The problem came several years later when cattle prices fell dramatically and the gift was cost-ing the IU Foundation substantial outlays of cash. The decision was made to sell the farm, and an investor group, intent on developing a toxic waste dump on the property, made an offer to purchase the land.

Local residents heard of the offer and began to protest the sale. In turn, IU students heard about the protests of the Mississippi citizens and began a very public protest in Bloomington. A symbolic barrel of toxic waste was carried to the IU president's office in Bryan Hall.

"Tom quickly came to my aid," Curt said, "and firmly suggested that we had to find another way to resolve the issue."

Tom, with no hesitation, told Curt, "This is not the right thing to do, compromising quality of life for citizens to solve a university predicament. You must consider alternatives."

Curt said that Tom's emphasis on pursuing what was right, from an ethical perspective, put in place the highest bar in decision-making. "With this kind of counsel—to pursue what was right and good for all parties in a conflict—we were encouraged to refuse the investor's offer and seek other alternatives," Curt said.

The second lesson from the same issue was equally substantial, Curt said: "Tom also taught me to disaggregate the problem we were facing. There were two issues here: the financial burden that the donor's gift had created for the IU Foundation and the possibility of a toxic waste dump being created with land that the IU Foundation would sell. So both the financial and ethical ramifications had to be addressed."

Eventually, the university sold the Mississippi property to a lesser offer because of the ability to sell other property, back in Indiana, that was also included in the original gift. That permitted the IU Foundation to clear the accumulated debt on the cattle farm. And, along the way, the IU Foundation developed a series of policies that permanently addressed gifts of real property, requiring astute evaluation of both value and potential liability.

"I learned so much from Tom Lofton," Curt concluded. "His wisdom—and his generosity to share his sensitive and wise counsel—were great gifts to me personally and professionally."

Many of the Endowment's religious initiatives came directly from Tom Lofton. He was a creative thinker, a deep thinker who studied and reflected, and then initiated new action. The idea for sabbaticals for clergy members is a good example of his thinking to address the need for vitality and renewal in the church.

William G. Enright
Board of Directors, Lilly Endowment

Over the tenure of Tom's leadership, Lilly Endowment was extraordinarily generous to higher education in the state of Indiana and to Indiana University.

It was not uncommon for the Endowment to address several different priorities in one grant and to sustain interest and support for initiatives over longer periods of time. For example, in 2003, the Endowment launched the Initiative to Promote Opportunities through Educational Collaborations to address two realities in the state of Indiana: a very low ranking in the percentage of the adult working-age population with bachelor's degrees and an overall decline in its national ranking in per capita income. Indiana's thirty-nine accredited colleges and universities received resources from Lilly Endowment to expand opportunities for their graduates to find meaningful employment in Indiana. The funding of these initiatives progressed through successive rounds in 2008 and 2013. In the end, the economic health of the state, higher education, and the people of Indiana benefitted from the grants.

The topics addressed by the Endowment's grants to higher education, naturally, covered the gamut of concerns that comprised the public agenda in Indiana and the country. Such complex issues as technology clouds, the need for encouraging private philanthropy, corporate partnerships, and life sciences research—for example—captured the attention of both the state's universities and Lilly Endowment. While the specific endeavor may have changed from season to season, the impact of the Endowment's work under Tom's leadership was to concentrate on the very causes and the very quality of life first addressed by the founders of the Endowment in 1937.

D. Susan Wisely, Lilly Endowment's retired director of evaluation, said that the Endowment's founders identified three charitable purposes in their charter: "Religion, education, and community development were aspects of a single mission: the cultivation of an educated, virtuous citizenry. Eli Lilly stated this mission in his own manner when he said, 'I would hope we could help improve the character of the American people.'" Improving character, the Lillys believed, eventually would lead to improved quality of life for a citizenry today and long into the future.

To Tom, that improvement of quality of life was lifelong work. "We take seriously the faith and responsibility that the Endowment's founders placed in its future leadership and are resolute to do all we can to perpetuate their values and ideals for generations to come," the executive message stated in the 2014 Lilly Endowment annual report.

Tom also acted personally to address those issues and concerns significant to him and Betty. They established, for example, a fund in the Indiana University School of Law that was named for Tom's father and intended for the school's dean to utilize for most urgent concerns. Betty explained the significance of what such undesignated giving meant to the Loftons in their personal philanthropy: "It seems there is rarely money for educational institutions to consider change or to pursue bright new ideas because of the sometimes very narrow, specific designations donors make for their gifts."

"I served on enough boards to see that schools and organizations would commonly get gifts that were dedicated to very defined purposes. Tom and I agreed that those groups, generally, had a much better idea of what needed to be done at their institutions than we did. So in addition to giving to scholarship funds, we often gave undesignated gifts to be used by universities for their best and most critical needs at that moment in time," Betty said.

A LIFELONG, HUMBLE WALK

Tom Lofton died at the age of eighty-six in 2015 in the city of his birth.

Tom and Betty's former pastor at Second Presbyterian Church in Indianapolis, Bill Enright, spoke at Tom's memorial service. He quoted Micah 6:8 as one of Tom's favorite Biblical scriptures and a code by which Tom lived: "He has shown you, O mortal, what is good. And what does the Lord require of you? To act justly and to love mercy and to walk humbly with your God."

That humble walk—acting justly and loving mercy—comprised Tom Lofton's life, Bill said. "It was supremely significant to Tom to honor the founders of Lilly Endowment. His sense of integrity was strong, and knowing and respecting the values of those who went before him was Tom's legacy at the Endowment."

In the Lilly Endowment annual report published after Tom's death, Clay Robbins paid tribute to his lifelong mentor: "Mr. Lofton's unrivaled intellect, wisdom, and profound sense of loyalty to the values of Lilly Endowment's founders at all times were evident in his guidance of the Endowment's affairs. A man of deep Christian faith, it was important to him that each year a significant portion of the Endowment's grants supported people in need, and he personally mentored and helped countless individuals facing challenges in their lives. He is irreplaceable, and we miss him greatly."

Tom—like Eli Lilly—believed that life starts right and ends right, if you get character right. And Tom, in my thinking, got character right. His was a grand fusion of faith, discipline, and responsibility.

Clay Robbins
Chairman, President & Chief Executive Officer, Lilly Endowment

A Commitment to Innovation

A
Commitment to
Places for Learning

BUILDING AND PRESERVING

THE CAMPUSES OF

INDIANA UNIVERSITY

Excellence in higher education requires physical facilities that will both accommodate and enhance the broad and varied activity of an institution. A university campus must pay attention to the smallest of spaces—an individual dormitory room or isolated study nook for a single student—as well as the lecture halls and arenas to accommodate thousands for ceremonial and athletic activities.

For Indiana University, the requirements for physical campus environments vary widely from campus to campus across the state and are influenced, of course, by size, academic programs, and geography. At Indiana University Purdue University Indianapolis (IUPUI), for example, there is critical need for proximity to state government and to the capital city's advanced health-care complexes. By contrast, in Richmond, home to Indiana University East, five buildings comprise the campus that serves more than 3,700 students in a small college-like environment. In Bloomington, the campus is 1,937 acres today and accommodates nearly forty-three thousand students.

From the most sophisticated cancer research laboratories to soccer fields and summer science camps, or from residence halls to libraries, health clinics, museums, and acoustically perfect performance halls . . . the places that comprise Indiana University are conceived, planned, constructed, and preserved to enhance the university's teaching and research missions on its eight campuses across the state of Indiana.

Photo: Chris Howell,
Herald-Times

GAYLE KARCH COOK

The Good Business of
Historic Preservation

Conversations with Gayle Karch Cook, co-founder with her husband, Bill, of Cook Group Inc., eventually come to an emphasis on place. It's a theme in her communication because place is ultimately important to Gayle.

Take, for instance, the small town of Bloomington, which Gayle talks about with great affection and pride. After their marriage in 1957, the Cooks lived in Chicago until coming to Bloomington in 1963. The tiny eastside apartment in which she and Bill began their business in Bloomington is a place marked with rich memories, caring for their newborn son, Carl, there and working until 1 or 2 a.m. on the books of the new business.

When Gayle and I first came to Bloomington, it was a sleepy, pretty place with a magnificent university. Our dream was born in this community. When the time came to move from Chicago, I asked Gayle if she would like to relocate and it took two seconds [for her] to say yes. Our lives were cast with this small city and large university. We have never looked back.

Bill Cook

Chicago's huge McCormick Place, site of the first radiology convention the Cooks attended to promote their medical devices, is one of those places that defined early the success the Cooks were to achieve. At a medical trade show there in 1963, Bill was using a Bunsen burner to demonstrate how to make a catheter from plastic tubing. Charles T. Dotter, MD, the Oregon physician who developed angioplasty, walked by and showed Bill how to refine the catheters to be used in widening an obstructed blood vessel. Dr. Dotter, who eventually become a lifelong friend of the Cooks, borrowed the burner, worked that evening, and made fifteen catheters, which Bill sold the next day for ten dollars apiece.

And, of course, there's the Indiana University campus in Bloomington, where Gayle earned her BA in Fine Arts, with Phi Beta Kappa honors. IU Bloomington was her first home-away-from-home and became a focal point of activity for the Cook family.

WANDERING INDIANA

When the young Cooks came to Indiana from Chicago, leisure time was a special commodity. Their new business of manufacturing wire guides, needles, and catheters was demanding. "I was the manufacturer and the sales department," Bill once said, "and Gayle was in charge of billing and quality control."

"We took Sundays off and drove all over southern Indiana, looking around and seeing things. We found all these interesting places and we kept notes," Gayle said.

Bill and I always liked Indiana history and architecture, and we spent hours exploring southern Indiana in the 1960s when we could spare the gasoline and the time. That was our recreation, eking out a few hours from our small Bloomington business.

Gayle Cook

Those Sunday drives brought back warm memories to Gayle. She grew up in southern Indiana, running and playing in the fields and farmlands around Evansville. "I don't really know why, but I've always liked old things—I've always seemed to be attracted to older buildings and older houses," she said.

There was, of course, not one specific day in her life when Gayle knew she would eventually become one of the most active historic preservationists in the history of the state of Indiana. But she does recall, as a young person, being attracted to what went before her in society and in her community. An urge to preserve, to restore, to rebuild—activities that define, in many ways, the dearest interests of her life—were to become, in many ways, her lifeblood.

Soon, for Gayle, the interest in places in her home state became more than a Sunday drive. Gayle started her first business in the early 1970s: *A Guide to Southern Indiana*, a guidebook that she designed, printed, promoted, and distributed from the Cooks' Bloomington apartment. The book went through five printings, each time updated with information Gayle and Bill had collected on their Sunday afternoon outings.

One Sunday drive was especially significant to Gayle. The Cooks were driving near Salem in southern Indiana and came upon an old grist mill, constructed in the 1800s and still standing with a waterwheel and milling machines intact. "We were fascinated by all the machinery, and it was so scenic, with the water still flowing. So we asked around and people told us to be careful," Gayle said.

A Commitment to Places for Learning

"Don't step on that property," the Cooks were warned. "The owner will come at you with a shotgun!"

But Gayle found the phone number of the family who owned the mill and called the owner one morning to ask if she and Bill could take a photo of the mill for the cover of the guidebook. "Sure," he said. So the Cooks drove down to Salem right away, and by the time they arrived, the owner was mowing the grass for the photo.

The first edition of the Cooks' guidebook, published in 1972, featured a photo of Beck's Mill. And thirty-five years later, the owner got his payback, Gayle explains: "We worked with the Friends of Beck's Mill—a nonprofit that the owner had donated the mill to—to restore it. We bought from the family seventy-nine acres of woods around the mill, so it's a park now. There are trails, good walks through the woods, and a beautiful waterfall."

Beck's Mill was added to the National Register of Historic Places in 2007, one of forty such projects the Cooks pursued in historic preservation. The projects ranged from a single building like the Carnegie Library in Bloomington to an entire town square, like Canton, where Bill was born in Illinois.

TOUCHING THE PLACE THAT IS INDIANA UNIVERSITY

The places Gayle and Bill Cook touched at Indiana University Bloomington—those spaces they helped build, remodel, and preserve—are sites for learning at IU that host the myriad activities comprising a major research university today.

Wylie House Museum

One project particularly close to Gayle's heart is the Wylie House Museum, built in 1835 as the home of Andrew Wylie, IU's first president, and restored in the 1960s. A two-story brick structure on an original twenty-acre farmstead, the house is located on Second Street just a few blocks from downtown Bloomington and the IU campus.

In the early 1990s, as leaders of the Indiana University Women's Colloquium, Gayle and Peg Brand, former Indiana University first lady, raised funds to purchase a period reproduction carpet for the Wylie House Museum. Carey Beam, director of the museum, said that "Gayle's support and invaluable counsel were critical to the successful completion of the museum's Education Center," adjacent to the historic house. Constructed in 2010 to provide IU instructors and students the opportunity to have immediate access to nineteenth-century artifacts, documents, and photographs, the center was named to honor Morton C. Bradley Jr., a distant relative of Andrew Wylie, in recognition of his estate gift.

The restoration and new construction on the Wylie farmstead resulted in a property that became a living legacy for today's generation in interpreting the early history and culture of both Indiana University and the town of Bloomington.

A Commitment to Places for Learning

The museum and its collections are resources for IU students in history, education, English, fine arts, apparel merchandising, interior design, gender studies, anthropology, public health, and music.

"Houses like this must be used and be relevant as significant places today," Gayle said. "What are we going to do with historic houses?" she asks. "There are something like fifteen thousand in the United States now, and each year there are many more added to the lists. Wylie House is one that is earning its keep."

The next Wylie project, in Gayle's mind, is addressing the accessibility of the house. "There was originally a two-story back porch, and if we can put that back on, with a ramp, the house will become accessible. That's part of getting the building ready so more classes can meet there and visitors can have physical access to the structure," Gayle said.

Mrs. Cook has been an unparalleled advisor to the Wylie House Museum. As a member of the Dean's Advisory Board, she volunteers her considerable expertise to help steer the museum's direction and offer essential guidance in preservation, an area not usually familiar to libraries.

Carey Beam
Director, Wylie House Museum,
Indiana University

Cook Hall

Place a photo of the Wylie House Museum alongside Cook Hall and you'll quickly see the breadth and variety of Gayle and Bill Cook's love for Indiana University. A basketball development center for the women's and men's basketball programs, Cook Hall is connected to Simon Skjodt Assembly Hall and characterized by all that is new and shiny in contemporary design.

IU's headquarters for basketball practice, training, and conditioning, the sixty-seven-thousand-square-foot, multilevel facility features practice courts, locker rooms, offices, meeting rooms, and Legacy Court, a display of the history of IU men's and women's basketball. Cook Hall was dedicated in 2010 as part of For the Glory of Old IU, the first capital campaign of Indiana University's Department of Intercollegiate Athletics.

The Cooks led the way in showing that athletics is a worthy beneficiary of major philanthropy. Their gift enabled us to build Cook Hall, with all the good things that have come from that. Most significantly, the two sides of Cook Hall, men's and women's, are mirror images of each other. That means our highest-profile women's sport is now on an equal footing with the men's. That is enormously important. Through the Cooks' generosity, women's basketball has become a bellwether for all the women's sports on campus.

Fred Glass
Vice President and Director of Athletics,
Indiana University

Cook Music Library

The William and Gayle Cook Music Library is one of the largest academic music libraries in the world, comprising more than seven hundred thousand catalogued items on 56,733 linear feet of shelves. The library occupies a four-floor, fifty-five-thousand-square-foot facility in the Bess Meshulam Simon Music Library and Recital Center.

Curt Simic explained the background of the naming of the music library: "It was after the construction of the library that we approached Gayle and Bill and requested their permission to name the new facility in their honor. It was clear that the new music library was a world-class resource, and even though the Cooks sought no public acknowledgement, we wanted to be sure that we recognized their contribution to such a significant stride forward for the Jacobs School of Music."

The Cook Music Library made it possible to bring the massive holdings of the Jacobs School of Music together in one place, including recordings and scores, and integrated analog and digital collections. The library houses special collections, including the Leonard Bernstein Collection, artifacts, scores, and memorabilia from perhaps the greatest American conductor and composer.

The Cook Music Library has distinguished the Jacobs School of Music far beyond the quality of the collections themselves. Unexcelled in size, the library has earned a reputation for developing technological advancements to fully serve constituents.

Before the Cooks' gift, the IU Music Library was known for its collections, but it was out of space, scattered among three locations. The new facility brought everything together. That was a major transformation, one that made the lives of the students so much easier. The other enormous improvement, of course, was in the technology. The Cook Music Library was designed from the outset to unite all the technological elements and make them accessible: scores, audio recordings, performance videos. The result? Unparalleled opportunities for students and faculty, and a world-class reputation that benefits us all.

Philip Ponella
Director, William and Gayle Cook
Music Library

ENCOMPASSING PHILANTHROPY

The broad philanthropic interests of Gayle and Bill Cook reflect, of course, the span of Indiana University. They gave scholarships and several endowed academic chairs in the Jacobs School of Music, School of Medicine, and School of Education and also endowed ten Wells Scholars.

In 2004, Cook Group Inc. was the benefactor of a named professorship in the Indiana University School of Medicine to honor Glen Lehman, MD, for his years of service to the field of gastroenterology and for his role in the development of instrumentation to enhance patient care.

Gayle said that Bill developed a fondness for the IU School of Medicine in their earliest days in business. "We were manufacturing products for brand new medical techniques back then, and the School of Medicine was on top of the technology. The school was performing the procedures so critical to the advancement of cardiovascular system study, and they liberally shared information with us to advance the development of instruments," Gayle said.

Most recently, in 2012, Gayle and her son, Carl, gave a lead gift to the Cook Band Building Fund to be used for the construction of the new Ray E. Cramer Marching Hundred Hall on the Bloomington campus.

> *If you listen carefully to people, they will tell you what is important to them. Gayle and Bill Cook were so multidimensional in their philanthropy because of their broad interests—music, athletics, medicine, historic preservation— all areas of human endeavor that they valued and honored with their giving.*
>
> *Curt Simic*
> President Emeritus, Indiana
> University Foundation

The degree to which philanthropic deeds are interwoven at an institution is, at times, both unexpected and curious. The Leonard Bernstein Collection in the Cook Music Library is a special tribute to the man who said he had "fallen in love" with the Indiana University music school when he spent six weeks in Bloomington to write his final opera, *A Quiet Place*. Upon his father's death, Bernstein's son said, "My father's artistic and educational connection with Indiana University was very strong. He adored the institution and became close to the dean, its faculty, and of course, its students."

In 1988, the Tanglewood Music Festival in Massachusetts was planning to honor Bernstein's seventieth birthday and asked the composer which of his compositions he would like to see performed. He suggested his *Mass*.

Charles H. Webb, dean emeritus of the Jacobs School of Music, explained that the Tanglewood staff told Bernstein that they did not have the resources to perform *Mass* because "the composition requires a huge orchestra, a jazz band, children's chorus, regular chorus, and ballet dancers." Bernstein, who had become intimately acquainted with the Jacobs School of Music by this time, said in response: "Why don't you call Indiana University?"

Charles continues, "After the performance—which involved two hundred and fifty IU students— Bernstein reportedly said, 'This is one of the greatest concerts I have ever heard.' He paused, and then went on to say, 'I don't just mean one of the greatest concerts of *Mass*, I mean of anything.'"

Gayle and Bill Cook have restored approximately sixty buildings, and forty-five of those generate income. "Preservation is good business," Gayle says. And she and Bill proved that on their very first restoration project, the Cochran House in Bloomington. The Cooks undertook the preservation of the building in 1976, the year that the National Trust was utilizing the motto "Preservation Is Good Business." And we thought, "Well, let's see if it is good business."

The Cooks needed a new standalone business site removed from the Cook Group headquarters, and the Cochran House, built in 1850 on the corner of Eighth and Rogers in downtown Bloomington, was in disrepair and threatened. "We decided to buy the house and see if it could be restored as economically as we could build a new facility," Gayle said.

"We got a quote on a new seven-thousand-five-hundred-square-foot building and kept record of all the work on the Cochran House, of every expense. Not just the building but also the lumber and the bricks and the draperies, the security system—everything in the building. It turned out to be more economical to restore it. That was a good example, so we thought, 'Well, we'll try it again,'" Gayle said.

Historic restoration, one of Gayle's grand loves in life, reached its zenith when the Cooks, in partnership with Historic Landmarks Foundation of Indiana, undertook the restoration of the French Lick Springs/ West Baden Springs resort. Gayle calls the work "the most massive and thrilling project" they ever accomplished, and in size, it was incomparable: two hotels, 3,200 acres of southern Indiana hills and woods, and three golf courses. And even in this, the largest of her endeavors, place was an important marker: "I have a 1910 photo of my grandmother at the French Lick Hotel and a 1925 photo of my parents at the West Baden Hotel," she said.

Is restoration good business? Both the hotels are on the National Register of Historic Places and Historic Hotels of America listing. The West Baden Hotel is a National Historic Landmark and a National Historic Engineering Landmark. The project received two Awards of Excellence from the National Trust for Historic Preservation. "I am sure that our family will never get to do anything like it again," Gayle said.

"IF I DON'T, WHO WILL?"

"I'm a little different from Bill because we had such different interests. I relate my projects to what I know about—buildings and architecture," Gayle explained. And she cites a most recent project at Indiana State University. ISU was renovating what was their library and discovered stained glass lying in the attic. The dome of the building had been completely dismantled, and a ceiling had been installed under the dome.

"I learned about it from a friend here in Bloomington, and I soon began to think that if the building could be restored, there would be a big central room again, open for students to use for reading and get-togethers," Gayle said. She pursued the restoration of the building and the dome. It was dedicated in 2015.

I'm really a pretty thrifty person. So I'm not one to throw money around. For me, I have to know something about the recipient. That's why the preservation projects have such an appeal to me, because I know what I'm doing.

Gayle Cook

"Pretty thrifty" is an apt description of Gayle Cook today. Since the death of her beloved Bill in 2011, Gayle has remained in Bloomington, living in the same home she and Bill purchased in 1967 when they moved from their first apartment.

What is Gayle's legacy at Indiana University, in the town of Bloomington, or around the state of Indiana? First, of course, she mentions places when she reflects on an answer to that question: "I think that sprinkled around the country are some buildings and someday, someone will walk into one of them and ask, 'Wow, I wonder where this came from?'"

"Someone may enter Wylie House Museum or West Baden or the Cochran House and hear those stories of restoration. They will look about and learn about the past. I think that's what happens when you make the surroundings more interesting and preserve some beautiful places and objects," Gayle said.

"And no one else is doing it. So if I don't, who will?"

Photo: Indiana University Foundation

V. WILLIAM HUNT

A Hoosier Legacy

Stories of V. William (Bill) Hunt's Indiana University memories and experiences flow from him with great emotion and affection.

He'll tell you about the first football game he attended at IU—he was but four or five years old and the Hoosiers were playing Iowa, he recalls. It was a beautiful fall day, and he's not sure, but "it might have been homecoming."

He remembers fondly his springtime trips as a high school senior to Bloomington for rush weekends and his family's trips to campus when they almost always stopped at the Indiana Memorial Union for lunch.

And his first business venture, a pick-up/delivery laundry and dry cleaning service he started as an undergrad. "A nickel a shirt, a dime for a pair of pants, and a quarter for a sweater," he says. "I actually financed my senior year with my earnings."

"My whole life has been associated with Indiana University," Bill says. "It's been a lifelong love affair."

IU AND FAMILY TIES

Bill was born with an IU—and a Hoosier—legacy. His father, Virgil Hunt, earned both his bachelor's and master's degrees in chemistry from Indiana University. In 1940, at age twenty-eight, Virgil became the youngest college president in the United States when he assumed leadership of Central Normal College in Danville, Indiana. Herman B Wells, then president of Indiana University, delivered an IU commendation at Virgil's inauguration.

Five years later, Dr. Wells revisited the young alum and asked him to establish an IU center in Kokomo to offer returning veterans a local opportunity for a university education. His father, Bill said, accepted the invitation and became "the chief cook and bottle washer, and the registrar, counselor, teacher, maintenance man . . . whatever was necessary to open the IU Kokomo Extension, as it was then called."

Bill and his sister, Marjo, soon became regular visitors to the extension in their Kokomo neighborhood. After school, the Hunt kids would stop by to see their dad at his office and then walk or bike on to their home a few blocks away.

About the time Bill finished the sixth grade, his father accepted another IU appointment, this time to become dean of the university's center in downtown Indianapolis, prior to the establishment of Indiana University Purdue University Indianapolis (IUPUI).

A GENERATION LINKED TO LEADERSHIP

The IU legacy continued for the Hunt family when Bill's sister enrolled at Indiana University in 1959 and Bill followed in the early 1960s.

Bill's springtime trips to Bloomington resulted in his moving directly into the Sigma Chi house as a freshman, and he rose up through the ranks of fraternity leadership each year, eventually becoming house president. One of his summer jobs put him in the office of the IU president and afforded him the opportunity to spend considerable time with Herman B Wells. The relationship with the beloved Dr. Wells had great impact on Bill, as it had had on his father, Virgil, in other days.

"Dr. Wells was as down-to-earth as you can get. He believed in creating opportunity for everyone and wanted to extend educational programming to reach all Hoosiers around the state. He epitomized the solid Midwestern values that I grew up with, and I developed the greatest respect for him both as an individual and as a public figure," Bill said.

Bill received his bachelor's degree in government in 1966 and his law degree from the Maurer School of Law in 1969. But his commitment to IU, at that juncture, was only beginning.

Like many of his classmates from the era, graduation wasn't an end for these young alumni but a gateway to lives of connection and service. They seemed destined early in life to stay linked with classmates and to welcome new responsibilities for leadership at their alma mater.

Curt Simic, president emeritus of the Indiana University Foundation, was director of the IU Student Foundation during Bill's junior and senior years at IU. Curt recalls the student leaders of the mid-1960s and how their service to IU was begun as undergraduates and nurtured through graduation into their lives as alumni.

"Men like Bill's brother-in-law and Sigma Chi brother John Biddinger, and Danny Danielson, J. Dwight Peterson, Mike Shumate, Dave Gibson—these were Bill's revered figures. He was among a group of distinguished individuals who stood out as student leaders and continued—and in many

There were two student organizations that left indelible impressions on Bill Hunt as an undergraduate at Indiana University.

The first was his fraternity, Sigma Chi. And his leadership training began the day he moved into the house. "You arrived with some thirty pledges and you're literally put in a room and challenged to self-organize. You're told some of the things you're going to be responsible for, such as room cleaning, hall cleaning, restroom cleaning, and wake-up calls—but you have a lot to figure out on your own."

"It wasn't a picture-perfect example of self-governance, but it was a formative experience for me," Bill says. "I was the pledge-class president, and it was the first time in my life I really had any serious responsibility for other people."

The Indiana University Student Foundation was the other cornerstone for Bill as an undergrad. As a Steering Committee officer, Bill had assignments to escort Indiana University Foundation directors when the board was on campus. "We picked them up and took them to their meetings around campus," he said.

"And it was amazing what we learned in the process. The IU Foundation directors were role models of philanthropy. They taught us, by example, about the importance and honor of giving back to IU," he said.

"No doubt, they became our models for success," Bill continued. "It seemed that being honored and respected by your university was an ultimate validation of success in life for the directors. And, for many of us, that became something we wanted to imitate."

situations, actually stepped up—their engagement with IU when they graduated," Curt said.

After his graduation from law school, Bill served as vice president of administration, general counsel, and, eventually, chairman and CEO of Arvin, Inc., a global manufacturer of automotive components based in Columbus, Indiana. He joined the IU Foundation Board of Directors in 1998, realizing one of the dreams of his undergraduate days.

His service to IU has been exceptionally broad and has spanned three campuses of the university. He was a special advisor to President Myles Brand and President Adam Herbert and a member of the IU Kokomo Advisory Board, the IUPUI Board of Advisors, the Maurer School of Law Board of Visitors, the Kelley School of Business Dean's Advisory Council, the Eskenazi Museum of Art National Advisory Board, and the Indiana University Health System Board of Directors, which he eventually chaired.

In 2011, Bill was honored by his alma mater with the honorary Doctor of Humane Letters degree, bestowed to him at commencement on the campus in Kokomo that his father was instrumental in founding.

COMPLETING THE CIRCLE

"When I married Bill, I married IU, too. And I'm thrilled with both."

So Nancy Bergen Hunt, who graduated from Florida Southern College and then earned her master's degree at Butler University, describes her own dedication to Indiana University. In 2001, Bill and Nancy made a major gift to IU Kokomo that symbolized the Hunt family legacy of helping build—from the ground up—a strong Indiana University.

The Hunts' gift was for the construction of the state-of-the-art Virgil and Elizabeth Hunt Hall, a science facility with classrooms, laboratories, and administrative and faculty offices at IU Kokomo.

On a smaller campus, one building can have a tremendous impact on the work of an academic department, according to Patrick Motl, PhD, associate dean of the School of Sciences and associate professor of physics at IU Kokomo.

Patrick, who completed postdoctoral research at the University of Missouri, University of Colorado, and Louisiana State University, believes that Hunt Hall offers, frankly, "the best labs and classrooms I've worked in on any college campus." He explains that, often, science labs and facilities are aged and cobbled together. Working in a new facility that is designed for science rather than being converted from other uses is a distinctive feature that helps IU Kokomo be more attractive both to prospective students and prospective faculty, Patrick said.

Patrick is also one of the science faculty who teach in the Science Rocks Summer Camp, now in its ninth consecutive year at IU Kokomo. Meeting all afternoon for eight days, the camp is designed for middle school students from the local community.

"This is an important time for students," Patrick explains, "because at this age, they tend to lose interest in science."

The memory is a vivid one for Bill Hunt.

"Probably the greatest contribution I made to Dr. Wells was that I was his driver in the summer between my second and third years of law school," Bill explains. "And I got a chance to sit in the front seat next to one of the truly great human beings," he adds.

"We were walking to the car one day, and Dr. Wells said to me, 'Bill, I believe I'll drive today.'"

So Herman B Wells, then chancellor of Indiana University, drove, and his student driver rode shotgun. "From behind Owen Hall, we went down through what are now the Sample Gates, up Indiana, across Seventh Street to Woodlawn and then to his house on Tenth Street," Bill recalls.

It was late summertime, and summer school was over, so there was no one on campus. "I mean, if he tried, he wouldn't have been able to hit anyone, I think," Bill says.

"To our knowledge, this is the last time he ever drove his block-long Buick Electra 2.25," Bill says.

And they arrived safely. But the next day, when Bill showed up for work, he encountered Dr. Wells's assistant, who was quite unhappy that the chancellor had driven, and even more unhappy with Bill for letting it happen.

"When I got to the office, I just caught hell," Bill recalls.

"But who was I to question? He said he was going to drive."

"It makes a big impression when we welcome these kids from the community to our campus and are able to spend time in the labs of Hunt Hall with them. They quickly catch our excitement about astronomy, ecology, geology, or one of the other sciences we help them experience during the camp," Patrick said.

"I've been in the Science Rocks program long enough now that I meet students in high school, for example, who announce that they are going to college to study a certain science," Patrick explained. "It's not uncommon for them to say that their interest was first prompted in Science Rocks camp at IUK."

"I hope the Hunts get a chance to reflect on how many lives their gifts have touched. Students come to us here at IU Kokomo and bring, of course, all their big goals and dreams. Because of gifts from people like the Hunts, we are able to help some of those students begin to move toward realization of their dreams and plans," Patrick said.

Philanthropy is about believing in the mission of what the institution does. . . . It's about the person who believes in you and believes in your institution as much as you do and partners with you and walks with you and tries to achieve those goals. That's what Bill and Nancy do here.

Susan Sciame-Giesecke
Chancellor, Indiana University Kokomo

After becoming acquainted with Indiana University, Nancy accepted an invitation to join the National Advisory Board of the Eskenazi Museum of Art, and, in 2010, she became a founding member of the IU Women's Philanthropy Council. The council has become a national university model for engaging women in volunteerism and philanthropy.

Bill's interests, because of his own experience, are similarly broad. The Hunts support the Eskenazi Museum of Art and the IU Student Foundation, of course. But their generosity has extended to the Well House Society and the Maurer School of Law, among other designations.

In 2008, the Hunts created the V. William and Nancy B. Hunt Scholarship in the Maurer School of Law, designed for Indiana residents who did their undergraduate work at one of the eight campus of Indiana University. Bill explained the rationale behind the scholarship gift: "Top students are very much in demand in today's world, and that competition makes the availability of scholarship packages more important than ever. It's our hope that this gift will help Indiana Law continue to attract Indiana's brightest future lawyers and business leaders."

BACK HOME IN KOKOMO

Today, Bill returns to Kokomo often. He's sure to be there each year for commencement, he says.

"To feel that continuing sense of connection is important to me, so I spend time on the Kokomo campus during commencement. I like to meet some of the new graduates and hear family members talk about their great pride and enthusiasm at what their daughters or sons have accomplished," Bill said.

A Commitment to Places for Learning

In addition to spending time with IU Kokomo students, Bill always makes it a point to visit with faculty and staff when he's on campus. He and Nancy are supporters of the Virgil Hunt Service Awards at IU Kokomo, which honor faculty and staff for excellence in serving students and the entire campus community.

"Choosing to give back to your alma mater—to me—is one of the most direct links to what has made your success in life possible," Bill says.

"Indiana University was so meaningful to me. It was not a life-changing experience. It was my life," he said.

People come to volunteerism and they come to philanthropy from lots of places. For Bill and Nancy, they come to it because they really get the good that Indiana University does in the world. They understand what it does for our state, and they understand what it does for the world. And they have always been there for us.

Lauren Robel
Provost and Executive Vice President,
Indiana University

Dear Hunt Family:

I am humbled and honored to receive the 2017 Virgil and Elizabeth Hunt Scholars Program scholarship.

My name is Mary-Matalyn (Mattie) Tom and I graduated from Carmel High School. I hope to someday become a postdoctoral researcher and eventually a patent attorney. My passion is to help find a cure for diabetes, a disease that has plagued my family for many generations.

I am spending my summer as a Project STEM intern at the Indiana University School of Medicine/Glick Eye Institute. I will be researching the effects of race, gender, and diabetes under the direction of Brent Siesky, PhD. I am looking forward to gaining knowledge and making a positive impact on the lives of others on a global scale.

As a bio-chemistry major, I want you to know that I will bring my skills to IU Kokomo where I can build on my foundation. I promise to pay forward all opportunities I have been given. I will work hard to implement teachings and to ensure the Virgil and Elizabeth Hunt legacy of education, diversity, and social responsibility lives on through future generations.

With much respect and kindness,
Mary-Matalyn Tom
STEM Intern
Eugene and Marilyn Glick Eye Institute
Indiana University Kokomo

Photo: Samerian Foundation

CINDY SIMON SKJODT

A Family Love Affair with Indiana University

My love for this great institution has never been a secret. Every time I'm on this campus, I have an overwhelming sense of pride."

So Cindy Simon Skjodt talks about Indiana University, her undergraduate alma mater and the alma mater of her three children, Samantha, Erik, and Ian.

And the alma mater of her brother, David, and her sister-in-law, Jackie. And the alma mater of her cousins and several second cousins. "We've had more than twenty members of the Simon Skjodt family who attended or graduated from IU. It is a very family thing," Cindy said, speaking of her lifelong Indiana University connections.

Family linkages, family influences, family traditions—for Cindy, they form an extended network that dates back two generations in Indiana. Cindy's maternal grandparents immigrated to Indianapolis from Turkey, and her father, Mel, moved to the city from the Bronx in 1954 when he was stationed at Fort Benjamin Harrison.

It was in Indianapolis that Cindy's parents met and were married. Mel, who had completed both his bachelor's and master's degrees at the City College of New York, went to work as a leasing agent in Indianapolis after his discharge from the Army, earning one hundred dollars per week.

In 1960, Mel founded Melvin Simon & Associates with his brothers, Herb and Fred, and began to transform the shopping center industry by developing enclosed regional malls. In 1993, Simon Property went public as the world's largest real estate investment trust.

A giant, pure and simple, and a citizen in the noblest sense of that word. When the US Army sent young Mel Simon to Fort Ben instead of anywhere else, it was one of the greatest breaks the state of Indiana will ever get.

Mitch Daniels
Former Governor of Indiana; Current President, Purdue University

THE SIMON HERITAGE

Cindy, who today leads the private Samerian Foundation in Indianapolis, remembers her parents as giving people. "My mother, Bess, was a most compassionate person," Cindy said. "She gave so generously of what she had. She often sang at the synagogue, with such a beautiful voice, and she had incredible love to give us."

The gifts of her mother were memorable ones noted in the community, as well. Cindy tells the story of shopping one day with her son, Ian, in Indianapolis after her mother's death. They were approached by a stranger who recognized Cindy and said, "You're Bess's daughter, aren't you?"

"Yes, I am," Cindy responded. The stranger nearly broke into tears as she told Cindy about how wonderful her mother's voice was. "My mother gave of her talent, and she gave from her kind, kind heart," Cindy said.

Mel's generosity to the state of Indiana began early in his professional life, and "he understood and com-municated to us the importance of giving back," according to Cindy.

My father inspired me many years ago to take pride in my community, to help lift up others, and to recognize that giving financially is just as important as giving of your time and attention.

Cindy Simon Skjodt

It's not surprising that giving to Indiana University, for the Simon family, became a family affair and was focused on strengthening community at Indiana University. The first family gift, for example, honored Cindy's aunt and established the Helene G. Simon Hillel Center at IU Bloomington.

Through the generosity of Fred Simon and other private donors, and in memory of Helene G. Simon, Fred's wife, the current home of Indiana Hillel was dedicated in 1993 and became an important Jewish home-away-from-home for IU students. The center's mission is to assure that Jewish college students have opportunities to recognize and develop leadership skills and express their faith in both traditional and creative ways in a university setting.

Shortly thereafter, Mel Simon, in honor of Cindy's mother, Bess Meshulam Simon, gave a lead gift to build one of the treasures of the Indiana University Jacobs School of Music for devotees of performance. Other Simon family members joined the patriarch, Mel, in giving that resulted in the Bess Meshulam Simon Music Library and Recital Center. The cen-

A Commitment to Places for Learning

ter features two performance venues that have been called "a little piece of paradise for music lovers," Ford-Crawford Hall and Auer Hall.

Dedicated in 1995, the Bess Meshulam Simon Music Library and Recital Center houses the departments of music theory, musicology, music education, bands, and recording arts. There are several classrooms in the structure, as well as the William and Gayle Cook Music Library.

FAMILY GIVING

With families that become involved in larger philanthropic endeavors, the first gifts are many times the ones that are closest to their hearts, according to Curt Simic, president emeritus of the Indiana University Foundation. "A family's first priority is, often, the desire to honor or memorialize a family member," Curt said. "As their giving capacities grow and their interests expand, these donors continually ask themselves, 'What more can we do to improve the world?'"

For the Simon family, this evolution in giving led to the construction of a new facility that would become the flagship research building for the life sciences at Indiana University Bloomington.

Simon Hall houses faculty researchers from many different disciplines and encourages interdisciplinary study in structural biology, biochemistry, bioanalytical chemistry, bioorganic chemistry, biophysics, nanobiology/nanofabrication, biocomplexity, microbial biochemistry, and molecular virology.

Flad Architects, the Madison, Wisconsin, architectural firm focused on university science and research centers, was retained by Indiana University, under the leadership of Vice President Emeritus Terry Clapacs, to design Simon Hall.

The firm's description of the building reveals the immense task planners and builders undertake when they begin to conceive and build a contemporary facility that will be nestled among time-honored campus landmarks.

Modern science laboratories act as the crossroads for a community of the world's brightest minds. This is what Indiana University envisioned with Simon Hall. . . . Conceived as a unifying hub, Simon Hall is strategically placed at the intersection of the chemistry, biology, and biochemistry departments. . . .

Surrounded by historic structures, Simon Hall takes visual cues from neighboring Myers Hall, a 1930s *art moderne* building that was originally home to the medical school. Simon Hall echoes Myers in its isolated symmetry, and works in unison to complete it. By creating tension between the buildings, the relationship between them is reinforced. Aesthetically it fits with the distinctive limestone buildings and collegiate gothic architecture on the Old Crescent, creating a dialogue with the existing structures by sharing an architectural language.

In the spirit of the nearby chemistry building, which is adorned with chemical symbols and snippets of the periodic table, and Myers Hall, itself decorated with medical and biological symbols, Simon Hall's designers integrated symbols of the type of work which takes place inside.

Conceived by faculty, translated into clay by sculptor Amy Brier, and carved by Indiana Limestone Co., Inc. artisans, renderings of organisms important to geneticists adorn stonework near windows and doors. Visual grace notes on the edifice include the e-coli bacterium, a fruit-fly, an ear of corn, a paramecium, and a mouse skittering up the wall toward the lintel where a limestone depiction of the RNA code is installed.

As with other gifts, multiple Simon family members contributed to the construction of Simon Hall, which was dedicated in 2007. The benefactors of the building included Melvin and Bren Simon, Herbert and Bui Simon, David E. and Jackie Simon, Deborah J. Simon, and Cindy Simon Skjodt and Paul Skjodt.

The 140,000-square-foot Simon Hall is home to more than 220 researchers and several instrumentation facilities related to such capabilities as DNA sequencing, nuclear magnetic resonance, and biological mass spectrometry.

Simon Hall received *R&D Magazine's* 2008 honors for its architecture in the "Lab of the Year" competition. The building, constructed of four thousand tons of Indiana limestone, is connected to Jordan Hall, Myers Hall, and the Chemistry Building.

NEW SPACE FOR THE RESEARCH AND TREATMENT OF CANCER

The advancement of scientific research was epitomized in the Simon family's next gift to Indiana University. In a monumental step forward to address cancer prevention, diagnosis, and treatment, the Indiana University Melvin and Bren Simon Cancer Center opened in 2008 on the campus of Indiana University Purdue University Indianapolis (IUPUI).

The gift from Mel and Bren Simon resulted in the renaming of the IU Cancer Center and dramatically enhanced the patient care facility. It also established the Joshua Max Simon Cancer Research Fund, a research endowment in memory of the Simon's son.

A partnership between the Indiana University School of Medicine and Indiana University Health, Simon Cancer Center is the only National Cancer Institute–designated cancer center in the state of Indiana. It also is home to the world's only healthy breast tissue bank. Researchers at the Simon Cancer Center have made discoveries that have altered or defined treatment for testicular cancer; gastrointestinal cancer, including pancreatic and colon cancers; genitourinary cancer, including germ cell tumors and bladder and prostate cancers; hematologic disorders, including multiple myeloma and leukemia; thoracic cancer; and thymoma and thymic carcinoma.

Mel Simon was one of the most generous people I've ever met; his passion for helping others forever changed the central Indiana community and improved the lives of thousands of people here and across the country.

Charles R. Bantz
Chancellor, Indiana University
Purdue University Indianapolis

A Commitment to Places for Learning

Following the death of her father in 2009, Cindy Simon Skjodt continued the model she learned from her parents of giving to honor family. The Melvin Simon Chair in Philanthropy, given by Cindy in 2013 in honor of her father's generosity, is one of six endowed faculty chairs at the Indiana University Lilly Family School of Philanthropy.

The purpose of the chair is to attract and retain world-class faculty members to advance philanthropy to improve the world.

"Education was important to my father," Cindy said. "It gives me so much personal pleasure to honor him, with the hope that I am able to inspire my children, family, friends, and others to give back and truly understand the need and the importance of being philanthropic."

Led by Mel's example, Cindy and the Simon family are models for thoughtful, effective philanthropic leadership. They are generous, forward-thinking partners of Indiana University and many other organizations, and they inspire others to greater generosity.

Gene Tempel
Founding Dean Emeritus, Indiana University
Lilly Family School of Philanthropy

Mel Simon shared a lifelong love of sport with his kids. Basketball, the Indiana sport of sports, was particularly important to him.

Mel purchased the Indianapolis Pacers with his brother, Herb, in 1983 and turned the franchise into one of the most respected in professional sports. For Cindy, her father's engagement with professional basketball presented an opportunity to create and lead a major philanthropic endeavor in Indianapolis, Pacers Foundation, Inc. In 1993, she became a founding director of the foundation, which is the public charity of Pacers Sports and Entertainment and is committed to improving lives of young people in Indiana.

Cindy has fond memories of seeing Indiana University basketball games in Assembly Hall both as a youngster and during her IU student days. "I grew up going to IU games and have great memories of watching basketball games with my father," Cindy said. "The atmosphere in Assembly Hall is truly unmatched anywhere in college basketball," she added.

In 2013, Indiana University was at a critical juncture with its esteemed basketball program and the iconic Assembly Hall. The hall was in essential need of updating and remodeling. The choice was to level the beloved hall or enhance what had been there since 1971 and had become one of college basketball's best-known and most-envied venues.

IU vice president and director of athletics Fred Glass and the Indiana University administration chose to build on the hallowed place, not destroy it.

Indiana University Athletics asked Cindy Simon Skjodt to consider a gift that would fund the remodeling, including new accessible seating, new restrooms, refurbished seats, new safety railings, a new video board, new escalators, new premium seating and hospitality areas, and substantial infrastructure improvements.

Cindy's one of us. She went to games as a little girl with her dad. She was a student here. She's been a season ticket holder. She's from one of the most philanthropic and sports-minded families in the state of Indiana.

Fred Glass
Vice President and Director of Athletics,
Indiana University

Ground was formally broken on April 7, 2015, and the massive remodeling went remarkably fast. Assembly Hall was reopened and dedicated October 14, 2016, as Simon Skjodt Assembly Hall.

"From the start, the goal of this renovation was to preserve the best home-court advantage in college basketball," Fred Glass said at the dedication ceremony. "As we stand here today, I trust you'll agree that we've not only preserved it, but we have dramatically enhanced it," he added.

At the dedication, Cindy expressed, again, her family's love for Indiana University. "Everyone in our family has enjoyed incredible experiences with Indiana University," she said. "We feel fortunate for our IU relationships, and it is rewarding to give back."

Today's event ushers in a new era in the history of one of college basketball's most iconic and venerable venues. This beloved building, which has been home to three national men's basketball championship teams and where millions have enjoyed so many unforgettable experiences, has been transformed in a way that both respects its storied history and ensures that the next generation of Hoosier fans will be able to grow their own memories in a safe, comfortable, exciting, and enjoyable environment.

Michael A. McRobbie
President, Indiana University, at the Dedication of Simon Skjodt Assembly Hall, October 14, 2016

PASSING THE LEGACY ON

There are two great loves in Cindy Simon Skjodt's life: family and the city of Indianapolis. With Paul Skjodt, whom she married in 1987, she has reared her three children in Indianapolis, the city in which she too was reared.

Following the legacy of her philanthropic parents, Cindy's career today is, truly, philanthropy. And it is her intention to assure that this legacy is passed forward to her own children through the family's Samerian Foundation.

Samantha, Erik, and Ian—whose first names were used to create the name Samerian (Sam-er-ian)—are members of the Samerian Foundation Advisory Council. Cindy dedicates her time, leadership, and financial resources to central Indiana, invests broadly in the city of Indianapolis, and is often called upon to lead philanthropic initiatives. Most recently, she was appointed by President Barack Obama to the United States Holocaust Memorial Council.

And the legacy, if Cindy's hopes are realized, will continue into the next generation of Simons: "I look forward to sitting in this iconic basketball hall and watching people share good times, experience winning seasons, and create warm memories like I was lucky enough to enjoy as a young girl coming to games with my father."

And then she pauses, smiles, and adds, "Go Hoosiers!"

Following
On Any Given Sunday. It's early January, cold and snowy outdoors. Purdue is in town. And the IU Women Hoosiers beat their perennial rival Boilermakers in Simon Skjodt Assembly Hall. After the game, senior captain Tyra Buss is surrounded by autograph seekers at center court.
Photo: Indiana University Athletics

Afterword

Stories—whether simple or complex, brief or elaborate—often find niches to inhabit in our hearts and minds. We treasure and retell the best stories, of course, in hopes of keeping close that which inspires, entertains, or informs us.

When Curt Simic and I began this work nearly three years ago, we committed to tell the stories of thirteen of Indiana University's alumni and friends whose lives are characterized by generosity. The group we selected could have easily numbered fifty or a hundred, because there is an almost unlimited number of donors whose relationships with IU epitomize the spirit of giving that we hoped to capture.

To learn more about the benefactors we selected and to explore their dreams as philanthropists, Curt and I did something that we both still love to do: sit with people and listen to their stories.

Across a dining room table in New York City, we heard Lucie Glaubinger speak of the importance of touching people through philanthropy. Clay Robbins sat with us in his Indianapolis office and spoke about the influence of his lifelong mentor, Tom Lofton.

Down in Franklin, Indiana, we went to lunch at Bob Evans with Mary Margaret Webb. We were in the restaurant only a few minutes when a former student of Mary Margaret's came to our table and thanked her for being such a "terrific" teacher.

Pat Miller had sandwiches ready for us, and as we sat on her porch for lunch she talked with enthusiasm about the *next* gift she and Mike would make to IU. Sid Eskenazi told us about Uncle Naphtali's gifts that made an Indiana University education possible. Cindy Simon Skjodt described her family's multiple IU linkages and her rich memories of going to Assembly Hall with her dad to watch Hoosier basketball.

In Curt's office on the Bloomington campus, David Henry Jacobs talked about the day his mother asked him a simple question: "What would you like for your birthday?" Gayle Cook told us about how she and Bill learned, firsthand, that remodeling and preserving places is good business and that historic houses can earn their keep in today's world.

And so here, we share the stories we heard. New stories at times—but familiar ones too—about thirteen people whose lives capture the spirit of generosity. We learned, anew, about the beauty of simple acts of giving and how that giving can bring about good at a place called Indiana University.

The stories inspired us. May they also resonate with you as new lessons of giving continue to evolve in our lives.

As we were finishing this work, good news came of a landmark gift to Indiana University from two of Indiana's most generous philanthropists, Sidney and Lois Eskenazi. The announcement underscored our perception that giving—to and for Indiana University—is robust, strong, and dependable precisely because it is most commonly motivated by dreams of achieving a greater good.

Reflecting their lifelong love of art and their large love of IU, the Eskenazis gave to fund new student scholarships, exceptional academic programs, and vital scholarly research in the newly named Sidney and Lois Eskenazi School of Art, Architecture + Design.

To this spirit of generosity, to inspired dreams of immense good, we say, with Herman B Wells, "Onward."

Sandra Bate
January 2018
Bloomington, Indiana

Curtis R. Simic is president emeritus of the Indiana University Foundation. During his twenty-year presidency, he is credited with boosting voluntary giving from $70 million and 60,000 donors to more than $270 million from 120,000 donors annually. A national leader in institutional advancement, he has mentored hundreds of advancement professionals who now lead fundraising in American higher education.

Sandra Bate directed the marketing and communications initiatives at the Indiana University Foundation and the Indiana University Alumni Association. During her career in advancement at Indiana University, she also served at Indiana University South Bend, Indiana University Purdue University Indianapolis, and the School of Public and Environmental Affairs at IU Bloomington.